Alpine Trailblazer is dedicated to
preserving the irreplaceable
bounty that nature
has bestowed upon
this unspoiled California
mountain community.

Hope Valley

"I only went out for a walk,
and finaly concluded
to stay out till sundown,
for going out, I found,
was really going in."
                    - John Muir

ALPINE TRAILBLAZER
Where To Hike, Ski, Bike, Pack, Paddle, Fish
In And Around Alpine County

second revised edition

text by Jerry Sprout
photographs and design by Janine Sprout

For Carrie, Jerry, Lea and Al

ISBN 0-9670072-0-8

Library of Congress Catalog Card Number: 99-90115

Diamond Valley Company, Publisher
89 Lower Manzanita Drive
Markleeville, CA 96120

trailblazer@gbis.com

Printed in the United States of America on recycled paper
Copyright ©1999 by Jerry and Janine Sprout

Thanks to Paula Pennington, Jim Dunn, Kate and Richard Harvey, Joan Wright, Greg Hayes, Jack Lewin, the
Rob Moser family, Heidi Hopkins, Patty and John Brissenden, Cynthia and Michael Sagues, Matthew Sagues,
Tim Pemberton, Edie Paulson, Elsa Kendall, Richard Hawkins, Tim Gillespie, Georgia and Vic Sagues, Carol
Mallory, Jim Rowley, Nicole Rowley, Barbara Howard, Linda Kearney, John Manzolati, Lutgarda Gutierrez,
Ellen Scott, Joe Stroud, Chet Carlisle, Marge and Jerry Purdy, Suzanne and John Barr.

cover: Markleeville Peak from Charity Valley

ALPINE

Trailblazer

WHERE TO

HIKE SKI BIKE PACK PADDLE FISH

IN AND AROUND ALPINE COUNTY

JERRY & JANINE SPROUT

DIAMOND VALLEY COMPANY

MARKLEEVILLE, CALIFORNIA

PUBLISHERS

TABLE OF CONTENTS

MAPS

INTRODUCING THE ALPINE SIERRA

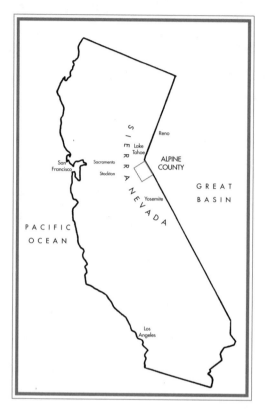

The Sierra Nevada forms the eastern border of California, 200 miles from the Pacific, a 400-mile wall of peaks averaging 70 miles wide and more than two miles high. An impenetrable barrier to the Spaniards who named it "Range of Snow" in 1776, the Sierra today has the world's longest system of interconnected mountain trails.

On its west side, the range rises gently to its crest over a distance of 50 to 65 miles, up from near sea-level valleys that span the midsection of California. From its crest toward the east is a different story: The Sierra Nevada drops abruptly in 5,000- to 7,000-foot escarpments into the valleys of the Great Basin high desert.

Because of the Sierra's geographic and topographic features, a trip across the width of the range from the Great Valley to the Great Basin is one through widely diverse ecosystems—from streamside woodland to yellow pine belt, through mixed conifers and subalpine belt, over the treeless crest, through the Jeffrey and piñon pine belts and into the sage lands of high desert. In this 60- to 80-mile, west-to-east trip, climactic and biological features vary equivalent to that of a north-south range from northern Mexico to the fringes of the American Arctic.

Of the nine Sierran automobile passes above 6,000 feet, six are within or bordering Alpine County—Echo, Carson, Luther, Ebbetts, Monitor, and Sonora. Alpine is the trans-Sierra gateway partly due to topography. Glacial and volcanic features folded together here, making for anomalous breaks in the range of peaks. But Alpine was also the historical route choice due to rich gold and silver deposits in the Mother Lode, Comstock Lode, and several other strikes, that beckoned emigrants and entrepreneurs by the tens of thousands from 1850 through the early 1900s.

The Sierran wall gets taller as you go from north to south, with peaks averaging around 7,000 feet in the northern region, elevating to 11,000 feet in Alpine County. Generally, the range is more arid as you go south, with the exception of "the Pineapple Express," winter storms from the South Pacific hitting the California coast.

The Golden Gate, the mouth of the San Francisco Bay, is a break in the Coastal Range west of Alpine that acts as a door for Pacific storms that drop rain and snow, increasing in volume as air rises, to a maximum downpour at an elevation of 6,500 feet on the west slope. In the hundred-odd years since records have been kept, the greatest snowfall was recorded at Tamarack Lake in Alpine County, a depth of 73.5 feet. Storms are mostly spent as they cross the Sierran Crest, with some 20 inches of rain on the east slope at 5,500 feet, compared to almost quadruple that amount at the same elevation on the west side. Thus, the aridity of the Great Basin combines with Pacific storms, sun with water, providing Alpine with optimum conditions for mountain flora and fauna.

What the Pacific bequeaths, the Sierra only partially returns. From high-mountain origins, rivers such as the American, Mokelumne and Tuolumne flow westerly to the ocean, on the way providing irrigation to farms that supply the

Jeff Davis Peak

nation with its fruits and vegetables, and San Francisco with its drinking water. Much of the melted snow, however, flows east of the crest, in the Walker, Carson and Truckee rivers, headed to a system of east Sierra lakes and finally to the alkaline sinks of the Great Basin. The Alpine Sierra is the origin of several rivers that drain both east and west, including the Truckee which fills Tahoe.

Alpine was made a county in 1864, when silver deposits were discovered in the area. Until that time, most of Alpine was thought to be part of the Nevada Territory. Wishing to avoid losing more riches to Nevada, the California Legislature resurveyed the State's eastern border, getting the land officially into the Golden State. It then created Alpine County by biting off chunks of the high country from five existing counties—Amador, El Dorado, Tuolumne, Calavaras and Mono. The result of this geographic pastiche is a county uniquely diverse in its scenery and natural features.

The name "Alpine" was chosen because Scandinavian miners and others who had been to Europe thought the region's grassy river valleys with surrounding forests and snow-capped peaks were much like the Alps. Alpine is also apt because the Pacific Crest Trail runs through the center of the county, and much of it is above the tree line, the very definition of "alpine." You might also call this "Alpine" because of Snowshoe Thompson, Alpine County's mountain expressman. In 1854 he fashioned the first downhill skis in America and as mail carrier crossed the Sierra for a decade before the railroad was completed. Snowshoe Thompson put on displays of downhill derring-do, perhaps setting then land speed records, and later engaged in competitions that were the origins of alpine skiing.

Alpine County is 775 square-miles, 95 percent of it public land. It's population of about 1,000 is by far the smallest in the state, and far fewer than the number of cows, deer and a number of other resident mammals. The county has more campsites than homes, even factoring in the major ski resorts at Kirkwood and Bear Valley. All highways are official scenic routes, and traffic control consists of a blinking yellow light at Woodfords.

In this book you will find 71 trailheads in the Alpine Sierra around Hope Valley and Markleeville—with day excursions to Tahoe and Yosemite. These trails lead to several wilderness areas—Carson Iceberg, Mokelumne, Desolation, Hoover, Ansel Adams—as well as the Tuolumne Meadows area of Yosemite National Park, and three National Forests—Toiyabe, Stanislaus and El Dorado.

Alpine has several major rivers, dozens of streams and creeks and peaks, and more than 60 high-mountain lakes. It's topography includes polished granite, volcanic plugs, slate-topped peaks, mountain meadows, hot springs, alpine ridges, and sage-belt piñon forests. With its mountain passes and Forest Service spur roads that go north and south, Alpine gives access to the interior of the Sierra toward all points on the compass.

Western White Pine near Granite Lake

DRIVING TO AND AROUND ALPINE COUNTY

ALPINE COUNTY FROM:

San Francisco Bay Area	3.5 to 4 hours	Stockton	2 hours
Sacramento	2 hours	Reno	1.25 hours

Above cities are closest commercial airports.

LOCAL DRIVE TIMES

Markleeville to Hope Valley: 20 minutes

Markleeville to:		Hope Valley to:	
Grover Hot Springs	10 minutes	Carson Pass	10 minutes
Monitor Pass	25 minutes	Minden/Gardnerville	25 minutes
Gardnerville/Minden	30 minutes	Meyers	25 minutes
Ebbetts Pass	35 minutes	South Lake Tahoe "Y"	35 minutes
Stateline Tahoe	1 hour		
Bridgeport	1.5 hours		
Yosemite			
Tioga Entrance	2 hours		

All highways in Alpine County are officially designated State Scenic Highways.

THE PASSES

Echo Summit (7382') Hwy. 50, South Tahoe to Sacramento
Luther Pass (7740') Hwy. 89, Hope Valley to South Tahoe
Carson Pass (8573') Hwy. 88, Hope Valley to Sacramento/Stockton
Kingsbury Grade (7334') Hwy. 207, Tahoe to Carson Valley
Monitor Pass (8314') Hwy. 89, Markleeville to Hwy. 395 (closed in winter)
Ebbetts Pass (8730') Hwy. 4, Markleeville to Stockton (closed in winter)
Sonora Pass (9628') Hwy. 108, Bridgeport to Stockton/Modesto (closed in winter)
Tioga Pass (9945') Hwy. 120, Yosemite east entrance (closed in winter)

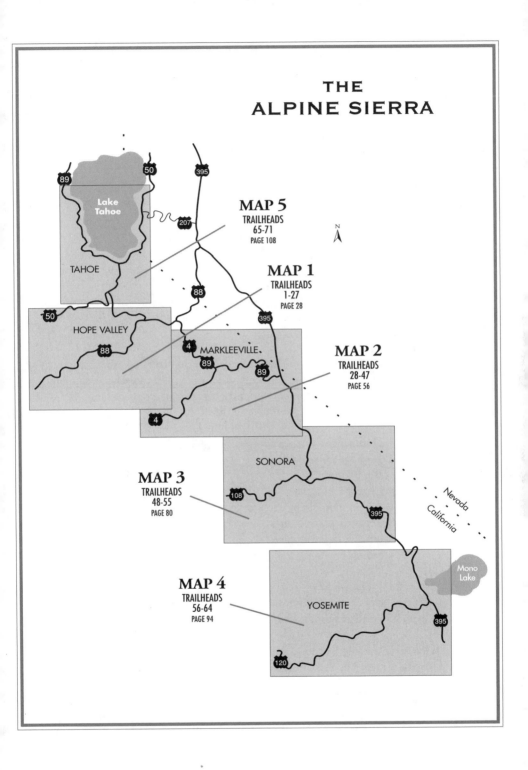

THE
ALPINE SIERRA

MAP 5
TRAILHEADS
65-71
PAGE 108

MAP 1
TRAILHEADS
1-27
PAGE 28

MAP 2
TRAILHEADS
28-47
PAGE 56

MAP 3
TRAILHEADS
48-55
PAGE 80

MAP 4
TRAILHEADS
56-64
PAGE 94

Lake
Tahoe

TAHOE

HOPE VALLEY

MARKLEEVILLE

SONORA

YOSEMITE

Mono
Lake

Nevada

California

N

KEY TO READING TRAILHEAD DESCRIPTIONS

Note: All distances are round-trip, except as noted for car-shuttles.

---

23. TRAILHEAD NAME   **ACTIVITIES BANNER**
    Best for:
    Park:
    Maps: (S A M P L E)

H:

BP, MB, CC, B, F

"23." Trailhead Number. These correspond to numbers shown on the five Trailhead Maps. There are 71 trailheads. Numbers begin on Map 1, Hope Valley, and get bigger as you go south. Exception: the Tahoe excursions, which are north of Hope Valley, are last in the sequence *(Map 5, Trailheads 65-71).*

Trailhead name. This is where you park to begin hikes and other activities. Some activities take place at the trailhead, for instance, a kayak or fishing spot. For other activities, such as cross country skiing or mountain biking, the trailhead is a destination, as is noted in the descriptions.

Activities banner for this trailhead. Each trailhead is suitable for one or more of the following activities.
    H = day hiking
    BP = backpacking
    MB = mountain biking
    CC = cross country skiing
    B = boating *(kayaking, canoeing, rafting, sailing)*
    F = fishing

Best for: Notes what is special about this trailhead and what in general to expect. Specifically mentions wildflowers, fall color, horseback riding and swimming, when appropriate.

Park: Gives directions to parking. Corresponds with trailhead number on regional map. The map for each region precedes its trailhead descriptions.

Maps: Lists U.S. Geological Survey 15-minute topographical map(s) for this trailhead. Most hikes in this book can be done without a topo map, but maps are recommended for longer hikes and off-trail hiking. Resource Links section in back of book gives sources for obtaining maps.

H: The first paragraph following the **H** symbol gives hike destinations, length of hike in miles, (miles off-trail, if any, in parentheses), and total elevation gain in feet.

The second paragraph following the **H** symbol gives brief directions to each destination. The first mention of a **Hike Destination** is boldfaced. Closest destinations come first, followed by those places further along the same trail. Described next are destinations on trails which fork from the original trail, or begin on a different trail from the same trailhead. Stay on marked trails to reach destinations, unless directions specify options.

BP, MB, CC, B, F: Below the hiking directions are the letter symbols for the activities for this trailhead. Directions for each activity follows each symbol.

ESTIMATING THE TIME FOR A HIKE IN TWO STEPS

You can estimate the time it will take to complete a hike by knowing its length and elevation gain—and how fast you want to walk.

> Example: How long will it take to hike to High Lake and back?
> **H:** High Lake, 6 mi., 1000 ft.

STEP ONE

For an average-conditioned hiker at average speed:
Divide the total miles by 2
6÷2 = **3 hours**
For a better-conditioned hiker going at a fair clip
Divide the total miles by 3
6÷3 = **2 hours**
For a less-conditioned hiker making steady progress
Divide the total miles by 1.5
6÷1.5 = **4 hours**

STEP TWO

All hikers add .5-hour for every 1000-foot elevation gain.
1000-foot hike = .5 hour
The time to High Lake will be 2.5, 3.5 or 4.5 hours, depending on the hiker.

Recommendation: Before beginning, calculate the number of hours a hike will take by using the above method in order to make sure you don't run out of daylight—or giddyup!

TRAILHEAD DIRECTORY

H = day hiking
BP = backpacking
MB = mountain biking

CC = cross country skiing
B = kayaking, canoeing or other boating
F = fishing

HOPE VALLEY
Trailheads 1-27, Map 1

MARKLEEVILLE
Trailheads 28-47, Map 2

SONORA
Trailheads 48-55, Map 3

YOSEMITE
Trailheads 56–64, Map 4

TAHOE
Trailheads 65–71, Map 5

Above Tuolumne Meadows

THE BEST OF THE ALPINE SIERRA

TH = Trailhead. *See pages 12-14 to find page number of trailhead description in book.*

Best for Day Hikers—

TOUGH PEAKS

Raymond Peak, TH19

Silver Peak, TH35

Highland Peak, TH39

Dicks Peak, TH66

Pyramid Peak, TH68

EASY PEAKS

Elephants Back, TH4

Leviathan Peak, TH46

Lembert Dome, TH62

BIG VIEW PEAKS

THAT STAND ALONE

Hawkins Peak, TH21

Big Sam, TH50

Sonora Peak, TH51

Mount Hoffman, TH64

Mount Tallac, TH66

TAHOE RIM PEAKS

Waterhouse Peak, TH1

Stevens Peak, TH2 or TH3

Jobs Sister, TH25

Freel Peak, TH25

PEAKS WORTH THE CLIMB

BUT FEW DO

Markleeville Peak, TH16

Reynolds Peak, TH19

Careys Peak, TH23

Thompson Peak, TH26

Tryon Peak, TH39

CLIFFS THAT ARE PLACES

UNTO THEMSELVES

Caples Creek Buttes, TH7

Thunder Ridge, TH11

Sorensen's Cliffs, TH22

Thornburg Canyon, TH30

LAKES WITH FEWER VISITORS

Shealor Lakes, TH9

Scout Carson Lake, TH10

Grouse Lake, TH18

Bull Lake, TH39

Asa Lake, TH40

Bull Run Lake, TH43

LAKES WITH GREAT VIEWS

Winnemucca Lake, TH4

Raymond Lake, TH19

Noble Lake, TH39

Summit Lake, TH56

Young Lakes, TH62

LAKES TUCKED

IN HIGH MOUNTAIN CRAGS

Crater Lake, TH2

Fourth of July Lake, TH4

Raymond Lake, TH19

Emma Lake, TH52

Granite Lakes, TH59

LAKES IN BUNCHES

Carson Pass South, TH4

Lower Blue Lakes, TH17

Virginia Lakes, TH56

Gaylor Lakes, TH59

Fallen Leaf, TH66

Lake Aloha, TH68

Best for Day Hikers (cont'd)—

FALLS AND CASCADES

West Carson Cataract, TH22
Horsethief Canyon, TH23
Grover Falls, TH32
Glen Aulin, TH61
Glen Alpine, TH66
Horsetail Falls, TH69

BEAUTIFUL PLACES
ON CLOUDY DAYS

Bagley Valley, TH45
Monitor Pass, TH46
Slinkard Valley, TH47
Mono Lake, TH57

HIKES WITH HISTORY

Devils Ladder, TH15
Horsethief Canyon, TH23
Silver Mountain City, TH39
Loope Canyon, TH44
Tallac Historic Site, TH65

HIKING ALONG THE
RIVER OR CREEK

West Carson, TH20
Pleasant Valley Creek, TH29
East Carson, TH32, TH37
Wolf Creek, TH36
Mokelumne River, TH41
Walker River, TH49
Little Walker River, TH52
Tuolumne River, TH60, TH61

OLD GROWTH CONIFER QUESTS

Horse Canyon, TH10
Devils Corral, TH18
Big Meadow, TH27
Upper Horsethief, TH23
Poor Boy Canyon, TH33
Peeler Lake, TH54
Mono Pass, TH57
Clouds Rest, TH63

SNOW-FREE IN LATE SPRING

Curtz Lake, TH28
Pleasant Valley, TH29
Grover Hot Springs, TH31
Hangman's Bridge, TH32
Poor Boy Canyon, TH33

MINE LOVERS
AND ROCK HOUNDS

Lost Cabin Mine, TH14
Silver Hill, TH34
Loope Canyon, TH44
Panum Crater, TH57
Great Sierra Mine, TH59

SHORT HIKES WITH SMALL KIDS
AND GRANDPARENTS

Frog Lake, TH4
Hope Valley, TH20
Curtz Lake, TH28
Pleasant Valley, TH29
Grover Hot Springs, TH31
Tallac Historic Site or
    Taylor Creek, TH65

Best for Fall Colors—

Scotts Lake, TH1
Red Lake, TH15
Charity Valley, TH16
Hope Valley, TH20
Sorensen's Cliffs, TH22
Willow Creek, TH24
Pleasant Valley, TH29
Wolf Creek South, TH36
Monitor Pass, TH46
Green Creek, TH55
Virginia Lakes, TH56
Kiva Beach, TH65

Best for Wildflowers—

EARLY SEASON, LOWER ELEVATION

Summit Lake, TH28
Pleasant Valley, TH29
Grover Hot Springs, TH31
East Carson Canyon, TH32
Poor Boy Canyon, TH33
Bagley Valley, TH45

MID-SUMMER, MID-ELEVATION

Lake Margaret, TH6
American River Potholes, TH8
Indian Valley, TH19
Horsethief Canyon, TH23
Big Meadow, TH27
Freel Meadows, TH26
Pacific Valley, TH42
Leavitt Meadows, TH49

Best for Wildflowers (cont'd)—

HIGH ELEVATION

Carson Pass, TH3, TH4
Devils Corral, TH18
Ebbetts Pass, TH38, TH39
Corral Valley Trail, TH48
Sonora Pass, TH51
Mount Hoffman, TH64
Mount Tallac, TH66

Best for Fishermen—

LARGER LAKES TO DRIVE TO AND FISH FROM A CRAFT

Silver Lake, TH10
Caples Lake, TH13
Blue Lakes, TH17, TH18
Lake Alpine, TH43
Twin Lakes, TH54
Virginia Lakes, TH56
Fallen Leaf Lake, TH66
Echo Lakes, TH68
Lake Tahoe, TH70

SMALLER LAKES TO DRIVE TO AND FLOAT TUBE

Woods Lake, TH14
Red Lake, TH15
Tamarack and Sunset Lakes, TH19
Burnside Lake, TH21
Indian Creek Reservoir, TH28
Kinney Reservoir, TH38

Best for Fishermen (cont'd)——

SMALL LAKES TO FLY-FISH
A SHORT HIKE FROM THE CAR

Scotts Lake, TH1
Crater Lake, TH2
Granite Lake, TH18
Summit Lake, TH28
Kinney Lake, TH38
Cooney Lake, TH56

FLY-FISHING STREAMS AND
RIVERS CLOSE TO THE CAR

Silver Fork of the
American, TH8
West Carson River, TH20
Pleasant Valley, TH29
East Carson River, TH32
Markleeville Creek, TH31
Mokelumne River, TH41
Walker River, TH49

FLY-FISHING
STREAMS TO DAY HIKE

Forestdale Creek, TH15
Wolf Creek, TH36, TH37
Pacific Creek, TH42
Mountaineer Creek, TH46
Slinkard Valley, TH47
Little Walker, TH52

BACKPACKING,
FLY-FISHING LAKES

Showers Lake, TH3, TH5
Fourth of July Lake, TH4
Emigrant Lake, TH13
Raymond Lake, TH19
Round Lake, TH27
Bull Lake, TH39
Bull Run Lake, TH43
Poison Lake, TH48
Anna Lake, TH52
Gilmore Lake, TH66
Middle Velma Lake, TH67
Lake of the Woods, TH68

Best for Mountain Bikers——

LAKE RIDES

Scotts Lake, TH1
Crater Lake, TH2
Blue Lakes, TH17, TH18
Wet Meadows, TH19
Burnside Lake, TH21
Indian Creek Reservoir, TH28
Highland Lakes, TH40
Fallen Leaf Lake, TH66
Lake Tahoe, TH65, TH70

HIGH-COUNTRY VIEWS

Forestdale Divide, TH15, TH18
Sorensen's Cliffs, TH22
Barney Riley Jeep Trail, TH32
Poor Boy Canyon, TH33
Loope Canyon, TH44
Monitor Pass, TH46

Best for Mountain Bikers (cont'd)—

LOOPS WITH HIGHWAY CONNECTION

Lower Blue to
Hermit Valley, TH17

Blue Lakes to Red Lake, TH18

Willow Creek to
Horsethief, TH24

Mr. Toad's Wild Ride, TH27

Curtz Lake to
Diamond Valley, TH28

Silver Hill to Bagley
Valley, TH34

Company Meadows to
Bagley Valley, TH46

RIDING AROUND ON

MOSTLY PAVEMENT

Kirkwood, TH12

Blue Lakes Road, TH17,
TH18

Ebbetts Pass Road, TH38

Monitor Pass, TH46

Tallac/Baldwin Beach, TH65

Tahoe City (Tour 6)

REGIONS TO EXPLORE BY BIKE

Wet Meadows, TH19

Burnside Lake, TH21

Horse Meadow, TH25

Wolf Creek Road/Dixon Mine,
TH37

Lake Alpine, TH43

Loope Canyon, TH44

Monitor Pass, TH46

Slinkard Valley, TH47

RIVER RIDING

Lower East Carson, TH32

Upper East Carson, TH38

Bagley Valley to Grays
Crossing, TH45

Buckeye Creek, TH53

Green Creek Road, TH55

Best for Backpackers—

OVERNIGHTERS AND KID TRIPS

Scotts Lake, TH1

Frog Lake, TH4

Lake Margaret, TH6

American River Potholes, TH8

Granite Lakes, TH10

Granite Lake, TH18

Indian Valley, TH19

Kinney Lakes, TH39

Duck Lake, TH43

TRAILHEADS WITH MANY

TRANS-SIERRA OPTIONS

Carson Pass, TH3, TH4

Wolf Creek, TH37, TH36

Ebbetts Pass, TH38, TH39

Highland Lakes, TH40

Little Antelope, TH48

Twin Lakes, TH54

Virginia Lakes, TH56

Fallen Leaf Lake, TH66

Echo Lakes, TH68

Best for Backpackers (cont'd)—

DESTINATION LAKES

Fourth of July Lake, TH4

Raymond Lake, TH19, TH39

Peeler Lake, TH54

Summit Lake, TH56

Gilmore Lake, TH66

Fontanillis Lake, TH67

Young Lakes, TH62

GOOD BASE-CAMPS

Meiss Lake, TH3

Round Top Lake, TH4

Wolf Creek, TH36

Bull Lake, TH39

Dumonts Meadow, TH37

Fish Valley, TH48

Upper Paiute Meadows, TH49

Glen Aulin, TH61

Lake Aloha, TH68

RIVER AND MEADOW CAMPS

Indian Valley, TH19

Horsethief Canyon, TH23

Falls Meadow, TH37

Silver King Valley, TH37, TH45

Pacific Creek, TH42

Fish Valley, TH48

Upper Paiute Meadow, TH49

Lyell Canyon, TH60

PACK 'N PEAK

Scotts Lake/

Waterhouse Peak, TH1

Round Top Lake/

Round Top Peak, TH4

Raymond Lake/

Raymond Peak, TH19

Indian Valley/

Reynolds Peak, TH19

Noble Lake/Tryon Peak, TH39

May Lake/

Mount Hoffman, TH64

Gilmore Lake/

Mount Tallac, TH66

Lake Aloha/Pyramid Peak, TH68

Best for Cross-Country Skiers—

MOONLIGHT RUNS

Kirkwood Meadow, TH12

Blue Lakes Road, TH18

Hope Valley, TH20

Grass Meadow, TH26

Hot Springs Meadow, TH31

JUST LEARNING CROSS-COUNTRY

Kirkwood Track, TH12

Hope Valley, TH20

Grass Lake Meadow, TH26

Bear Valley, TH43

Tallac Area, TH65

Fallen Leaf Lake, TH66

Best for Cross-Country skiers (cont'd)—

MODERATE DOWNHILL,
RELIABLE SNOW

Carson Pass North, TH3

Schneider Cow Camp, TH5

Kirkwood Cross-Country, TH12

Burnside Lake, TH21

Willow Creek, TH24

Horse Meadow, TH25

DOWNHILL RUNS/TELEMARKING

Crater Lake, TH2

Carson Pass South, TH4

Kirkwood Ski Resort, TH12

Forestdale Divide, TH15

Bear Valley Ski Resort, TH43

PLACES WHEN THERE'S
NO SNOW ANYWHERE ELSE

Carson Pass, TH3, TH4

Kirkwood, TH12

Red Lake, TH15

Bear Valley, TH43

Echo Lakes, TH68

PLACES TO SKI WHEN
THERE'S TOO MUCH SNOW
OR HEAVY STORM

Burnside Lake, TH21

Indian Creek, TH28

Pleasant Valley, TH29

Grover Hot Springs, TH31

Poor Boy Canyon, TH33

Best for Horseback Riding—

PLACES WITH
ORGANIZED PACK TRIPS

Kirkwood, TH12

Wolf Creek North/South,
TH37, TH36

Little Antelope, TH48

Leavitt Meadow, TH49

Tuolumne Meadows, TH61

RIVER AND STREAM RIDES

Pleasant Valley, TH29

Wolf Creek, TH36

Hermit Valley, TH41

Silver King, TH45, TH52

LAKE TRIPS

Scotts Lake, TH1

Lake Winnemucca, TH4

Blue Lakes, TH17

Tamarack and Sunset Lakes,
TH19

Indian Creek, TH28

Highland Lakes, TH40

VALLEY AND MEADOW

Charity Valley, TH16

Indian Valley, TH19

Horse Meadow, TH25

Bagley Valley, TH45

Slinkard Valley, TH47

HIGH COUNTRY VIEWS

Carson Pass North and South,
TH3, TH4

Forestdale Divide, TH15

Poor Boy Canyon, TH33

Silver Hill, TH34

Monitor Pass, TH46

Best for Kayaks and Canoes—

Best Swimming Holes, Small and Large—

Best Ways for Celebrating A Holiday—

FOURTH OF JULY

Wildflowers on
Carson Pass, TH3, TH4
Fireworks at Tahoe, TH65
Camping at Fourth of
July Lake, TH4
American River Potholes, TH8
Kayak Caples Lake, TH13
Drive Emigrant High
Country, (Tour 1)
Concert in Genoa, Nevada

LABOR DAY

Kayak and swim on
Silver Lake, TH10
Hike to Winnemucca
Lake, TH4
Cookout at Woods
Lake, TH14
Hope Valley concert at
Sorensen's Resort
Drive Bodie and
Mono Lake, (Tour 4)
Hike Raymond Lake, TH19

HALLOWEEN

Children's parade in
Markleeville
Fall color hike on
Monitor Pass, TH46,
Drive Alpine Mining District,
(Tour3)
Hike to Scotts Lake, TH1
Visitor center at
Taylor Creek, TH65
Nevada Day Parade in
Carson City
Hike Hawkins Peak, TH21

THANKSGIVING

Feast at Sorensen's
Hike Barney Riley Jeep
Trail, TH32
Bike or Hike Forestdale Divide,
TH15
Hike to Grover Falls, TH32

CHRISTMAS AND NEW YEAR'S WEEK, PRESIDENT'S DAY

Alpine skiing at
Kirkwood, TH12
Ski Red Lake, TH15,
Horse Meadow, TH25
or Burnside, TH21
Soak at Grover
Hot Springs, TH31
Moonlight ski
Hope Valley, TH20
Drive Comstock Lode, (Tour 5)

Best for Alpine Picnicing—

EASTER

Hike in Pleasant Valley, TH29

Bike Ebbetts Pass, TH39, or
Monitor Pass, TH46

Bike Indian Creek Reservoir
Loop, TH28

Stroll Hope Valley, TH20

Drive Tahoe Circle, (Tour 6)

MEMORIAL DAY

Visit Alpine County Museum
and Historical Complex

Raft the East Carson, TH32

Hike Horsethief Canyon,
TH23

Car camp and short
backpack trip

Drive Washo Country-Alpine
Valleys, (Tour 2)

SPOTS YOU CAN DRIVE TO

Kit Carson Road at
Silver Lake, TH10

East end of Caples Lake, TH13

Woods Lake, TH14

Faith and Charity
Valleys, TH16

Pleasant Valley, TH29

Alpine County Museum and
Historical Complex

Grover Hot Springs, TH31

East Carson River, TH32

Bridge at Wolf
Creek North, TH37

Lake Alpine, TH43

Monitor Pass, TH46

Centerville Flat Campground

Silver Creek Campground

Snowshoe Springs Campground

(see resource links for campgrounds)

REQUIRE A SHORT HIKE

Carson Pass, TH3, TH4

Charity Valley, TH13

Hope Valley, TH20

Willow Creek, TH24

Summit Lake, TH28

Pleasant Valley, TH29

Grover Falls, TH31

Hangmans Bridge, TH32

Wolf Creek South, TH36

Ebbetts Pass North, TH38

Monitor Pass, TH46

Bull Run Lake

Hope Valley

Stevens Peak

In the 1850s, the Emigrant Trail through Hope Valley was one of the world's main thoroughfares, the yearly route for 50,000 wagons to the California Gold Rush. In the decade that followed, during the even-richer Comstock Lode in Virginia City, the valley was also the corridor for eastbound silver seekers.

The Pony Express riders came through here too, after mounting fresh horses at a station in Woodfords. During the winter months up until the late 1860s, Snowshoe Thompson, the Norwegian emigrant who carried mail across the Sierra on homemade skis, was the only means of transportation through the Sierra. His route took him from the Carson Valley, up Woodfords Canyon into Hope Valley, over Luther Pass and finally, up Echo Summit and down to Placerville.

About a decade into the Comstock boom, the railroad route was completed over Donner Pass, some 60 miles away on the north side of Lake Tahoe. Local silver strikes continued to draw thousands through Hope Valley's high country until the 1870s, after which time it became off-the-beaten-path for most travelers. Little has changed since then. Only a few scars on granite from wagon wheels and the carvings on aspen by Basque sheepherders echo the valley's past. Hope Valley is center-stage for a large region that has retained its pristine nature due in part to the efforts of Friends of Hope Valley, Sierra Nevada Alliance and

Trust for Public Land, groups that have worked to promote conservation of scenic resources. The area is virtually all public land, including national forest and wilderness.

In the western reaches of the Hope Valley region are two large lakes, Caples and Silver, and dozens of smaller ones. West of the crest at Carson Pass are examples of glacial erratics—big rocks sitting alone, left behind by melting glaciers—and views toward the Sacramento Valley and a sense of the Pacific beyond. Through these granite fissures fall the headwaters of the American River. North and south of the Carson Pass are lakes and peaks of the Sierran Crest, an area which sees deep winter snow and a summer of wildflowers. The Pacific Crest Trail crosses Highway 88 at the pass.

East of the pass is the high meadow region, where a ring of peaks collect snow and send streams into Hope, Faith and Charity valleys. Blue Lakes lie above the valleys. This region was the site of several mining towns, now vanished, that were home for years to thousands of miners and the businessmen who fed off of them. The West Carson River forms here, meandering at first and then cascading through rugged Woodfords Canyon.

On the north side of Hope Valley is the Tahoe Rim, with peaks rising above mixed-conifer forests, from the tops of which are vistas contrasting Lake Tahoe with the high desert. Virtually every tree to be found in the Sierra Nevada grows within a ten-mile radius of Hope Valley, including a profusion of aspen that set autumn ablaze with color. National forest lands between wilderness areas have roads that can be used as tracks by mountain bikers and cross-country skiers, as well as for access by fishermen, hikers and horsemen.

Glacial Erratics

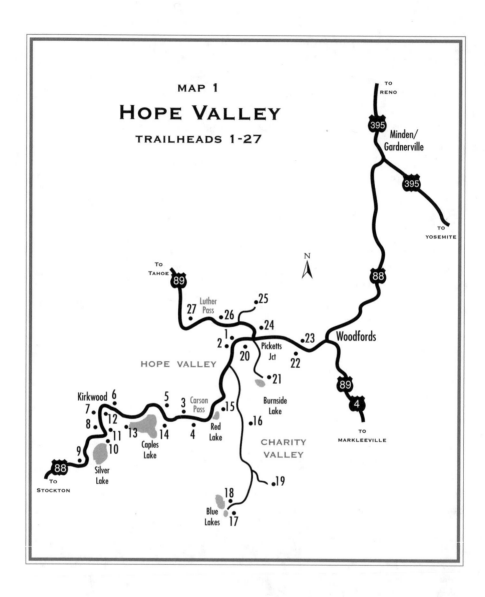

MAP 1

HOPE VALLEY

TRAILHEADS 1-27

TO RENO

395

Minden/
Gardnerville

395

TO YOSEMITE

N

88

TO TAHOE

89

27 Luther Pass

25

26

24

23 Woodfords

1

2 Picketts Jct

20

22

89

21

4

Kirkwood 6

5

3 Carson Pass

Burnside Lake

7

15

TO MARKLEEVILLE

8 12

16

11 13 14 4

Red Lake

CHARITY VALLEY

9 10

Caples Lake

88

Silver Lake

19

TO STOCKTON

18

Blue Lakes

17

HOPE VALLEY

TRAILHEAD DESCRIPTIONS

TRAILHEADS 1–27
MAP 1

H=Day Hiking, BP=Backpacking, MB=Mountain Biking,
CC=Cross Country Skiing, B=Boating, F=Fishing

1.   SCOTTS LAKE H, BP, MB, CC, F

Best for: Lake and peak combination, Tahoe and Hope Valley view, fall color, horseback trip or kid's backpack.

Park: Turn right, north, on unmarked Scotts Lake road, 1.25 mi. west of Picketts Jct.on Hwy. 88. Drive in about 1 mi., park at junction of a second road that joins from the south. At 7500 ft.

Map: Freel Peak

H: Scotts Lake, 3 mi., 500 ft.; Waterhouse Peak, 7 mi. (3 mi. off-trail), 2000 ft.

To reach **Scotts Lake**, follow the road through pine and aspen forest—a fall-color display—making switchbacks and then gradually ascending to the west. The lake is in the forested saddle south of the peak. To achieve **Waterhouse Peak** from Scotts Lake, go steeply, heading north/northeast from the lakeshore and avoiding impassible manzanita along the south slopes of Waterhouse. The trail follows a logging spur road for a while, but you'll need to go cross-country for the last mile or two, in a northerly direction as you approach the top. Note the avalanche chutes on the south face of the mountain—trees mowed down by the hundreds.

BP: Scotts Lake is popular among horsemen and also as a one-night trip for younger kids. Also a good choice for an autumn overnighter.

MB: Scotts Lake Road is part of a network of unmarked roads below Waterhouse and Stevens peaks, a recommended riding around spot.

CC: Good parking for Hope Valley moonlight skiing in the flats. During the day, ski to lake located at top of Scotts Lake Road, an infrequently used track.

F: Some fishermen come in by horseback to fly-fish for rainbows and browns in **Scotts Lake**.

2.   CRATER LAKE   H, MB, CC, F

Best for: Fall color, 360-degree alpine views, old mine exploration and dramatic cirque lake.

Park: Turn on unmarked Crater Lake Road, 2 mi. west of Blue Lakes Road on Hwy. 88. Although you can 4-wheel most all the way to the lake, hikers will want to park about 1 mi. in. At 7600 ft. *Note:* Another road, to Alpine mine, is .5-mi. east and is easily confused with Crater Lake road. Don't worry: These roads adjoin up higher, and both can be used to access Crater Lake or Stevens Peak.

Map: Markleeville

H: Crater Lake, 3 mi., 900 ft.; Stevens Peak, 6.5 mi. (3 mi. off-trail), 2400 ft.

To reach **Crater Lake**—an aquamarine pool beneath the steep walls of Red Lake Peak—walk up the road on its long switchbacks and take a fork to the left, one that does not cross the creek. The lake has been made larger by a cowboy dam at its eastern spillway. To reach **Stevens Peak**, take the right fork off the road, which crosses the Crater Lake drainage. From this crossing you can see the road climbing steeply toward Alhambra Mine. A second mine, Alpine, is .25-mile to the north of Alhambra. After making the hike up, leave the trail halfway between these two mines, picking a route steeply upward, headed westerly, on the south side of the peak. You'll reach the long, open saddle between Red Lake and Stevens peaks and see a trail that switchbacks up Stevens. *Note:* An alternate route to Stevens Peak is from Carson Pass North, TH3.

MB: Park at Hwy. 88, at either road described above. You can make a 6-mile, leg-burning loop via Alpine and Alhambra mines, and also take in Crater Lake.

CC: Finding where to park can be hard due to plow berms, but this area is little-used and offers great downhill runs through junipers and aspen. Southern exposure can make for sticky snow.

F: You can drive within .25-mile of **Crater Lake** or follow hiking instructions. Mostly brook trout.

3.   CARSON PASS NORTH   H, BP, CC, F

Best for: Wildflowers, fall color, "Sound of Music" majesty of the Sierra, vistas from horseback.

Park: At Carson Pass, Hwy. 88, north side of road just west of pass. A federal fee area. At 8500 ft. For car-shuttle leave second car at Big Meadow, TH27.

Maps: Silver Lake and Markleeville

H: Red Lake Peak, 4 mi. (some easy off-trail), 1400 ft.; Meiss Meadow, 5.5 mi., 800 ft.; Meiss Lake, 9 mi., 800 ft.; Luther Pass car-shuttle, 9 mi., 900 ft.; Showers Lake, 10.5 mi., 1200 ft.

All trails start west through aspen and junipers, with views of Caples Lake, and then turn north, across a drainage and up to a lakelet at the saddle above Meiss Meadow. From this vantage you'll see Tahoe to the north. To **Red Lake Peak**, take an unmarked trail just north of this lakelet/saddle, heading up the west slope of Red Lake Peak. Diagonal steadily upward to the saddle between Red Lake and Stevens peaks. (The trail continues to **Stevens Peak,** less than 2 miles, which gives a two-peak option for more energetic hikers.) Make your way up the north slope of Red Lake Peak. At the very top, you'll need to use your hands for the last, difficult 40 feet or so.

To **Meiss Meadow**, a green, flower-dotted expanse, continue north and down on the main trail from the lakelet/saddle. **Meiss Lake** is due north across the meadow, though you may wish to avoid boggy grassland by veering into lodgepole forest southeast of the lake—to your right as you approach. To **Luther Pass car-shuttle** take the trail from Meiss Lake's northwest shore, walking 1 mile northerly through undulating topography, reaching Round Lake. From Round Lake, head toward Big Meadow on the main trail.

To reach **Showers Lake**, stay on the west side of Meiss Meadow and take a left-forking trail before you reach Meiss Lake. The trail will climb north and west. *Watch out:* Since Showers Lake is in a different drainage, it's easy to lose the trail on the 1.5-mile trek up from the Meiss turnoff—get your bearings from the meadow.

Red Lake and Hawkins Peak

BP: Lots of day hikers, but packers will enjoy prime spots at Meiss and Showers lakes, as well as spots off Meiss Meadow.

CC: The schuss into Meiss Meadow is fantastic. Good skiing on shoulders of Red Lake Peak. The ski through to Luther Pass is recommended for experienced skiers on days with good visibility, but be prepared to take your skis off and post-hole the last steep mile through trees to the car at the Big Meadow parking area.

F: **Meiss Lake**, the source of the Upper Truckee, has cutthroat and some brook trout. Same species will be found at **Showers Lake**, a backpackers' choice.

4. CARSON PASS SOUTH H, BP, CC, F

Best for:	Wildflowers, knockout peaks and lakes, hiking and backpacking for all experience levels, horseback trips with views.
Park:	At Carson Pass, Hwy. 88, interpretive center and Snowshoe Thompson Monument. A fee area in summer and Sno-Park in winter. At 8500 ft. For Red Lake car-shuttle, park second car at Red Lake, TH15.
Maps:	Markleeville and Silver Lake

H: Frog Lake, 1.5 mi., 350 ft.; Forestdale lakelet loop, 8 mi. (4 mi. off-trail), 1800 ft.; Carson Pass to Red Lake car-shuttle, 6.5 mi. (1.5 mi. off-trail), 800 ft.; Winnemucca Lake, 5 mi., 600 ft.; Elephants Back, 7 mi. (2 mi. off-trail), 1100 ft.; Round Top Lake, 7.5 mi., 900 ft.; Round Top Peak, 8.5 mi. (2 mi. off-trail), 1900 ft.; Fourth of July Lake, 11 mi., 1900 ft.

Frog Lake, overlooking Hope Valley, is just the entry point to this area, but also a worthy destination. To reach the **Forestdale lakelet loop**, go about .5-mile south on the trail from Frog Lake and take the Pacific Crest Trail south, a left-bearing fork. The PCT goes around the north and then east face of Elephants Back. Then you hook south, off-trail, heading toward the visible upper part of the drainage, which holds the lakelet. To return, climb the shoulder above the lakelet, to the northwest, up to the top, which is the saddle between Round Top Peak and the Elephant. From there, you'll get the big view of Winnemucca Lake and of your route back. Contour to the north below Elephants Back, staying above the lake, until reaching the Winnemucca trail that takes you back. To **Red Lake car-shuttle**, go to the Forestdale lakelet, as described above, and from there go off-trail another .25-mile to the Jeep trail that leads back to Red Lake—you will be able to see the trail across the drainage from the PCT.

To **Winnemucca Lake**, one of the jewels of the Sierra, continue on the trail from Frog Lake. To top **Elephants Back**, walk up the dwarf sage-covered slope east and north of Winnemucca, a hike sturdy small kids will enjoy; this peak gives a big payoff for a small effort. **Round Top Peak** is that big huge thing towering south and a bit west of Winnemucca. To climb it, take the trail that leaves from the west shore of Winnemucca, climb a couple hundred feet, and then turn southerly, up one of several possible routes up the peak's northwest face. You'll reach a high saddle and walk toward the crags. Using your hands in spots, make your way around a false peak, which is just west of Round Top—and up to the peak itself.

Round Top Lake is about 2 miles west of Winnemucca. Continuing on the trail you depart to climb Round Top Peak through a granitoid saddle. **Fourth of July Lake**— which is surrounded by 2000-foot walls on three sides and 1000-foot drop into Summit City Creek at its spillway—is less than 2 miles south of Round Top Lake, but with more than a 1000-foot descent.

Watch out: Always take rain gear in Carson Pass area. Hail can appear quickly in the summer; lightning poses a threat at higher elevations. If you hear thunder, make haste to a lower elevation.

BP: Carson Pass South is well-used, but has many good camp sites. The Forestdale lakelet is a sleeper. Don't count on much firewood in this zone, due to use and sparcity of trees. Campfire restrictions will apply at higher elevations.

CC: The best skiing is toward Winnemucca from Carson Pass, and then down the bowl below Round Top Peak that leads to Woods Lake. Keep your bearings; from Woods Lake (in the woods), finding the eastward trail back to the pass can be confusing.

F: Most people walk into **Winnemucca Lake** for wildflowers and scenery. Not as many for the fishing, which is good for fishermen. Backpack to **Fourth of July Lake** for brookies and cutthroat.

5.   **SCHNEIDER COW CAMP**   H, BP, CC

   Best for: Alpine wildflowers, open vistas, family hike where volcanic meets granitic, skiing.
   Park: Off Hwy. 88 at Caples Lake, just west of road to Cal Trans. At 7900 ft. (Parking at Cal Trans lot rather than on the highway saves a little walking; ask permission, if open.) For car-shuttle, park second car at Carson Pass North, TH3.
   Map: Silver Lake

H: Schneider Cow camp, 4 mi., 600 ft.; Showers Lake, 12 mi., 2200 ft.; Meiss Meadow car-shuttle, 11 mi., 2000 ft.

Schneider Cow Camp, with its old barn and high ridge, is a good family walk or lunch spot. For **Showers Lake**, take the trail on the north side of the stream as it turns north from the cow camp meadow and climbs. On the way up you'll get views toward the west. Climb and hook east around an unnamed pointed peak and drop into Showers Lake. Returning via **Meiss Meadow car-shuttle** is a little easier walk back, provided you have a second car. Follow the trail from the east side of Showers Lake down to Meiss Meadow, where you will pick up the southbound trail to Carson Pass.

BP: Family trip to cow camp, or car-shuttle to Showers Lake.

CC: Schneider Cow Camp, behind a ridge, is a good cross country basin.
Watch out: Be careful of straying—the topography here can turn craggy higher up, with avalanche danger under and on cornices.

6. LAKE MARGARET H, BP

Best for:	Hidden-away lake, short backpack, variety of flora, including aspen and lush-loving wildflowers.
Park:	Look for turnout on Hwy. 88, just east of Kirkwood Cross Country Center. At 7800 ft.
Map:	Silver Lake

H: Lake Margaret, 4 mi., 300 ft.

Make sure to get on the right trail to **Lake Margaret**, as granitic knobs, many streams and flora create a maze difficult to navigate off-trail. Water-loving flowers will be tucked away in several choice spots along the way.

Meiss Meadow

BP: Above-mentioned features, plus a variety of lakelets, make Lake Margaret a choice for one-night backpackers.

7.   KIRKWOOD LAKE   H, B, F

Best For: Sunset view, scrambling granite, solitude on a busy day, swimming in isolated lakelets.

Park: Turn on Kirkwood Lake road, .5-west on Hwy. 88 from entrance to Kirkwood Meadows; look for turnout and trailhead within .25-mile on left. At 7700 ft.

Map: Silver Lake

H: Caples Creek Buttes, 6 mi. (3 mi. off-trail), 600 ft.

Before attempting **Caples Creek Buttes**, you may wish to take a gander from the Carson Spur, that precarious section of Hwy. 88 west of Kirkwood; from a turnout at the top is a full view of this multifaceted drainage. Study a route. At the trailhead, head downstream crossing Caples Creek after 1 mile, which can be problematic even in late summer, because flow is controlled by a dam. Make your way north-northwest, continuing to lose elevation—perhaps marking your path with stone piles—until walking out onto one of several granite promontories. From here are long views to the west, capturing fading daylight. Many swimming lakelets and mini-falls are in this area, though granite benches and brush make for deceptively difficult navigating.

B: Kirkwood Lake, just down the road from this trailhead, is a secluded high-mountain lake with a shoreline interesting for kayaking and canoeing.

F: Shore casting and float tubing in **Kirkwood Lake**.

8.   AMERICAN RIVER POTHOLES   H, BP, F

Best for: Wildflowers, cool off on a hot summer day in granite pools with falls.

Park: At Silver Lake Campground, 1 mi. east on Hwy. 88 from Kit Carson Resort Road at Silver Lake. Across highway from campground. At 7400 ft.

Map: Silver Lake

H: Along the Silver Fork of the American River, 4 to 8 mi., 500 to 1200 ft.

At the beginning, several campground trails and one Jeep road west of Martin Meadow head toward the **American River Potholes**. Your best bet is to find the river—the Silver

Fork of the American—and walk down on its north bank; you'll find the trail. The old road from Martin Meadow is about .5-mile east of the campground on Highway 88—this route doesn't join the river for about 2 miles. The potholes, natural pools scooped out of granite bedrock, begin about 1.5 miles from the campground. You can keep walking granite benches downriver, finding more pools and falls.

For the best wildflowers, including a profusion of purple delphiniums, walk back via the Jeep trail from Martin Meadows. This route is parallel to the river on the north—the old road bellies up and away from the river midway on the hike.

BP: Some out-of-the-way spots, with Roman-bath-like riverside campsites.

F: Fly-fishermen will have success on the **Silver Fork of the American** looking for rainbows and browns, especially in the fall when the campground has cleared.

9. SHEALOR LAKES H, BP

> **Best for:** Short day hike, one-night backpack, smooth granite, swimming in lakes and nearby lakelets.
>
> **Park:** Look for sign on Hwy. 88, 2 mi. west of Kit Carson Resort Road and spillway at Silver Lake. At 7700 ft.
>
> **Map:** Silver Lake

H: Shealor Lakes, 3 mi., 600 ft.

Shealor Lakes are on the main trail, drain into Tragedy Creek and the headwaters of the American River. A fun area to explore off-trail, as seven lakelets dot a mile-wide circle of glacier-polished granite. *Note:* Keep your bearings.

BP: Shealor Lakes are a destination for a kid's trip or a short getaway. You can find seldom-visited sites to pitch a tent.

10. SILVER LAKE H, BP, B, F

> **Best for:** Fire-and-ice hike from volcanic to granitic, wildflowers, old-growth junipers, waters of Silver Lake for swimming and kayaking.
>
> **Park:** At north end of Silver Lake, Kit Carson Resort Road, off Hwy. 88, 11 mi. west of Carson Pass. At 7300 ft.
> *Note:* Other trailhead parking for Horse Canyon is on Hwy. 88, 1 mi. east of Kit Carson Road.
>
> **Map:** Silver Lake

H: Granite Lakes, 4 mi., 200 ft.; Scout Carson Lake, 10 mi., 1300 ft.; Horse
Canyon view, 12 mi., 2500 ft.

To **Granite Lakes**, walk around the north shore and then down the east shore of Silver
Lake, past cabins and Campfire Girls Camp. The lakes are less than .5-miles south of the
water tank at the camp, about .25-mile east of Silver Lake's shore.

To **Scout Carson Lake**, pick up the trail as it skirts behind Kit Carson Resort, below the
volcanic cliffs at Silver Lake's northeast shore. You'll head southeast through red fir and
junipers—an unusually large forest of which extends up-slope from this area. Staying on
the trail, cross streams and walk out onto wildflower-dotted open slopes, leaving the volcanic world and entering the world of granite. Continue on the open trail, reaching Scout
Carson Lake. To **Horse Canyon view**, continue southeast from the Scout Carson Lake
and follow the trail as it drops steeply into the canyon, heading toward the deep drainage
of Summit City Creek. About 600 feet down from the trail's highest point, you'll reach a
trail that contours around the top end of Horse Canyon and takes you back up to the
Horse Canyon Trail, leading back out.

BP: Scout Carson is a very scenic lake; on busy weekends, expect company from
campers and cabin-dwellers at Silver Lake. Silver Lake trailhead can be a 2-night
car shuttle for backpacks to Caples Lake via Emigrant Lake, TH13. Backpackers
might also check in at Devils Hole Lake and Summit Meadow Lake, which are
within 2 miles southwest of Scout Carson, off-trail.

B: Silver Lake is one of the best for canoeing and kayaking. You can put in near Kit
Carson Lodge, or drive down Plasse Road, 2 mi. west on Hwy. 88 from Kit
Carson Road. Check out granite islands and channels at south end of lake.

F: Large browns and rainbows found by trolling deep around **Silver Lake's** islets.
Boat rentals available and canoe fishing is popular. Fly-fishermen may want to
float tube, since summertime brings shore-casters to the lake.

11.   THUNDER RIDGE   H

Best for:	Ridge-top panoramas, possible eagle sightings.
Parking:	At trailhead turnout on Hwy. 88, 2 mi. west of Kirkwood, just west of Carson Spur. At 8000 ft.
Map:	Silver Lake

H: Thunder Ridge, 7 mi., 1100 ft.; Thimble Peak, 10.5 mi., 1600 ft.

Thunder Ridge, a 4-mile long wall between Kirkwood and Silver Lake, begins with a
steady uphill walk through red fir and hemlock, climbing to the snow fences and eagle

Thunder Ridge

nest area above the dramatic Carson Spur. Continue south along the east side of the ridge, and then take a short series of switchbacks to its top—just beyond a route that leads down to Kirkwood. The trail continues south, jogging east and west of sub-formations piled on top of the ridge. You then come to an open area, with a long saddle south toward Thimble Peak. You'll find several volcanic knobs to walk up, including one furthest west that perches you on the 3000-foot cliff above Silver Lake.

To reach **Thimble Peak**—the landmark of Kirkwood's most challenging ski run—continue south along a sweeping saddle and up the peak's northwest face.

12. KIRKWOOD H, MB, CC

Best for: Explore ski slopes in summer with wildflowers and grassy ridges, cross country skiing and back country horseback trips.

Park: Turn at Kirkwood Ski Resort, off Hwy. 88, 6 mi. west of Carson Pass. Drive in 1.5 mi. to main ski lodge at southwest section of the valley. At 7600 feet. For car-shuttle park second car at Caples Lake, TH 13.

Map: Silver Creek

H: Thimble Peak loop, 7 mi. (3.5 mi. off-trail), 1800 feet; Emigrant Lake car-shuttle, 7.5 mi. (.75 mi. off-trail) 1000 ft.

For **both hikes**, the trail crosses to the east side of Kirkwood Creek and climbs to the northeast side of Thimble Peak ridge. Looping around and southward, to the backside of the ridge, you'll climb to the junction with the **Emigrant Lake car-shuttle** trail. To reach the lake, either contour west and south off-trail, or drop down toward Caples Lake and pick up the trail to Emigrant as it comes up from there. For the **Thimble Peak loop**—a circumnavigation—keep climbing a few hundred feet from the trail junction to the southeast saddle of Thimble Peak. At the saddle, leave the trail and contour around the south side of the peak, eventually coming around to views of Kirkwood from its highest and most notorious ski run. From here, traverse your way back down, bearing northwest and being mindful of precipitous cliffs.

MB: Park at the entrance to Kirkwood to explore the grounds of the resort. A leisurely ride of many miles, mostly on pavement, in a beautiful mountain valley.

CC: Kirkwood Cross County Ski Center, on the highway before you turn into the ski resort, offers rentals and some 59 kilometers of groomed trails for all experience levels. Telemark skiers also buy lift tickets at the downhill resort.

13.   CAPLES LAKE   H, BP, B, F

Best for: Wildflowers, midsummer day hike or short backpack, swimming and kayaking.

Park: At Caples Lake dam lot, .5-mi. east of Kirkwood on Hwy. 88. West end of lake. At 7700 ft. For Silver Lake car-shuttle, park second car at Silver Lake, TH10.

Map: Silver Lake

H: Emigrant Lake, 7 mi., 700 ft.; Silver Lake car-shuttle, 11 mi., 1500 ft.; Thimble Ridge loop, 10 mi., 2000 ft.

Two-thirds of the walk to **Emigrant Lake** is along Caples Lake's forested west shore. The trail then climbs and turns south into the Emigrant Lake basin. To take the **Thimble Ridge loop**, or **Silver Lake car-shuttle**, hike out of the lake basin, following the trail southward as it climbs steeply until reaching the shoulder of an unnamed peak due south and high above Emigrant Lake. The trail then drops over and down, reaching the Horse Canyon Trail after about .75-mile. Take that trail toward Silver Lake. **Car-shuttle hikers** stay on the trail all the way, for about 5 miles. **Thimble loop hikers:** One mile after reaching the Horse Canyon Trail, take a trail going north and up, to the saddle directly southeast of Thimble Peak. From the saddle, a trail drops down and joins up with the trail you came in on from Caples Lake.

BP: Packers to Emigrant Lake won't be disappointed, unless you forget mosquito repellant in July.

B: Canoeists and kayakers can put in at Caples Lake Resort for a fee, or for free on the west end of the dam, near the resort. The south end of the lake offers interesting channels and islets, and many spots for lunch and a swim.

F: Boat ramp at **Caples Lake Resort**. Fishing is good all day for brook, rainbow, brown and mackinaw trout. Boat rentals. Shore casting from spillway area at west shore.

14. WOODS LAKE H, BP, MB, CC, B, F

> **Best for:** Family picnic at lake with day hike, flowers, swim or paddle.
> **Park:** Take Woods Lake Road, 1 mi. west of Carson Pass on Hwy. 88. Drive in 2 mi. to lake. At 8200 ft.
> **Map:** Silver Lake

H: Round Top Lake, 3 mi., 1000 ft.; Fourth of July Lake, 6.5 mi., 2200 ft.
Note: Both these lakes are accessible via Carson Pass South, TH4.

The trail to **Round Top Lake** takes you immediately by historic **Lost Mine Cabin**, a photographer's favorite. Then you walk up along Round Top Lake's outlet stream, as it tumbles by watering nests of wildflowers. The trail to **Fourth of July Lake** is south from Round Top Lake, climbing at first and going down a 1200-foot ramp to the lake. Less energetic hikers can get a good look at the lake without going down.

BP: Both Round Top and Fourth of July lakes are excellent, popular choices.
MB: Roads into Woods Lake make for easygoing pedaling for the family.
CC: Park at Hwy. 88 and take the road in (noting there are two entrances from highway separated by about a mile). Winter wonderland-type skiing when snow is lacing the conifers.
B: Low-key canoeing and kayaking at Woods Lake, in the shadow of Round Top Peak.
F: Boat and shore fishing in **Woods Lake** for rainbow trout, accessible by car.

15. RED LAKE H, MB, CC, B, F

> **Best for:** Autumn hike, pioneer route, vistas from mountain bike or horseback, backcountry skiing.
> **Park:** Off Hwy. 88, at east end of Red Lake, 2 mi. east of Carson Pass. At 7900 ft.
> **Map:** Markleeville

H: Forestdale Divide, 8.5 mi., 1100 ft.; Faith Valley, 8 mi., 400 ft.; Devils Ladder, 3 mi., 600 ft.

The trail to **Forestdale Divide** can be driven from Blue Lakes, so hikers may encounter an occasional vehicle on summer weekends. About 2 miles in, heading south, you'll cross the bridge at Forestdale Creek, where the divide trail forks to the right. After climbing gradually southward to the top, you'll reach the divide, where westerly runoff heads for the Pacific Ocean and easterly for the Carson Valley. To get to **Faith Valley**, take the east-heading trail at the bridge on the way in; after two miles. You'll come to the confluence of Forestdale Creek and the West Carson River in Faith Valley. **Devils Ladder**, a nickname given to a horrendous segment of pioneer road east of Carson Pass, takes off from the parking area up the south shore of Red Lake to Carson Pass. *Local lore:* Although Red Lake, which is dammed, and modern roads have obscured some of the past, keen observers can spot wheel scrapes on granite and scars on trees from cables used to hoist wagons.

MB: Forestdale Divide to Blue Lakes, and a series of interconnecting Forest Service Roads (e.g. 013, 015, 081) in Faith and Charity valleys make this an area wide-open for mountain bike adventures.

CC: The bowl north of Forestdale Divide is a Nordic skier's dream, although snowmobiles may be encountered on busy weekends.

B: Canoeists and kayakers will enjoy paddling the smallish and scenic Red Lake.

F: **Red Lake** is accessible by car. Tube and boat fish the lake for trophy-sized brook trout known to frequent the inlet at the west end of the lake. Or stream-cast **Red Lake Creek,** flowing from the lake's eastern shore. In **Forestdale Creek**, 2 miles in, reachable by car, you'll find brook trout. Forestdale Creek flows into West Carson River, off Blue Lakes Road in Faith Valley.

16.   CHARITY VALLEY   H, MB, CC

Best for:	Group day hike, peak climb, wildflowers, fall color, horse and bike explorations.
Park:	Take Blue Lakes Road, off Hwy. 88, 3 mi. west of Picketts Jct. Go 6 mi., park on left near old log structure, just before pavement ends. For Jeff Davis Peak, park at turnout on left, 1.5 mi. south of old log structure. At 8000 ft. For Grover Hot Springs car-shuttle, park second car at TH31.
Map:	Markleeville

H: Grover Hot Springs car-shuttle, 7 mi., minus 1700 ft.; Markleeville Peak loop, 10 mi. (3.5 mi. off-trail), 1700 ft.; Jeff Davis circumnavigation, 6 miles (all off-trail), 300 ft.

The trail to **Grover Hot Springs car-shuttle** contours the gently sloping hillside, up and parallel to the dirt road that leads northeast out of the parking area. It dips and turns

West Carson River

through granite sand and mule ears, joining Charity Valley Creek at the east end of the valley. Not long after reaching the creek, the trail drops into upper Hot Springs Valley, and then follows Hot Springs Creek through mixed conifer forest and yellow-granite benches before reaching the meadow of the park. To get to **Markleeville Peak loop**, follow the road—not the trail—1.5 miles to where it crosses Charity Valley Creek, at a tumble-down bridge. The road turns easterly and then southerly as you walk up through forest, eventually coming in behind Markleeville Peak, on its northeast side. From here, at the open willowland of upper Sawmill Creek, make your way off-trail, westerly up the creek drainage. Hook northerly as you near the rounded top of Markleeville Peak. The descent is along the steep but safe southwest shoulder. Retrace your ascent route until about .5-mile south of the peak, and then drop steeply, headed west and veering north as you descend. You come down in the southern end of Charity Valley and walk the creek through the meadow back to the car. **Jeff Davis Peak** is the volcanic plug due south of Markleeville Peak. To walk clockwise around Jeff Davis, take off due east, headed for the notch in the saddle halfway between Markleeville Peak and Jeff Davis. Reaching the notch, you'll see Jeff Davis Creek below, headed east toward Pleasant Valley. Stay high, contouring in and out of Jeff Davis' volcanic outcroppings, and being mindful of steeper cliffs below you on the southeast side of the peak. You'll do a full circle at roughly the same elevation.

MB: A number of Forest Service roads interconnect in Faith and Charity valleys, making this an exploration zone for pedal-pushers. You can ride around a series of roads in the valleys, or connect with a road to Red Lake via Blue Lakes.

CC: Park at the entrance to Blue Lakes Road. The road, plus the open gentle slopes northwest of Markleeville Peak, make for good Nordic skiing. But be advised that snowmobiles frequent this zone, especially on weekends and holidays.

17. LOWER BLUE LAKE H, MB, CC, B, F

Best for: Canoeing, boat fishing, fall hiking, horseback riding and biking.

Park: Take Blue Lakes Road, 3 mi. west of Picketts Jct. Go 10 mi. (half unpaved) to Lower Blue Lake. Park at dam. At 8000 ft.

Map: Markleeville

H: Twin Lake, 1.5 mi., no elevation; Meadow Lake, 4 mi., 300 ft.; Evergreen Lake loop, 5 mi. (2 mi. off-trail), 700 ft.; Hermit Valley via Clover and Deer Valley car-shuttle 7 mi., minus 1100 ft.

Large **Twin Lake** is an easy walk to the southwest of Lower Blue Lake—although snow tends to linger in the shaded forest. The trail to **Meadow Lake**, through pine and fir, extends westward from Twin Lake. The cowboy dam at the west end Meadow Lake offers a pleasing sunset view.

To **Evergreen Lake**, follow the drainage that spills into Meadow Lake at its northeast shore. Walk up, off-trail, for 1 mile to the lake. To return to the trailhead, loop east and south from Evergreen Lake until rejoining the trail at Twin Lake. The trail (Jeep road) to **Clover Valley, Deer Valley** and **Hermit Valley** on Hwy. 4, takes off due south from the trailhead parking. Since the driving distance between Blue Lakes and Hwy. 4 is so great, hikers might also opt for an in-and-out to Deer Valley instead of a car-shuttle.

MB: Bikers might share the road from Blue Lakes to Hermit Valley with an occasional Jeepster. Terrain and rocks make this a challenging ride through a slice of beautiful country. A very long loop is possible by taking Highway 4 down to Markleeville and Highway 88 back up to Blue Lake. In the spring, Blue Lakes Road, beginning at the turnoff on the highway, is often snow-free and car-free, due to snow higher up at Blue Lakes; scenic pavement pedaling possible.

CC: Although Blue Lakes Road into Faith and Charity valleys is a good beginners' ski track, snowmobiles may make this a poor choice, particularly on weekends. Blue Lakes is a better Nordic choice for storms, weekdays, and moonlight skates.

B: See boating notes for Upper Blue Lake, TH18.

F: **Lower Blue Lake** and **Twin Lake** have small boat access for trolling. The lakes are heavily stocked, providing a good chance of landing a trout. Float-tube casting is popular in **Meadow Lake**. Look for rainbow and cutthroat.

18. UPPER BLUE LAKE   H, BP, MB, B, F

Best for: Hidden backpack lake, old-growth red fir, wildflowers, biking and horseback.

Park: Take Blue Lakes Road, 3 mi. west of Picketts Jct. Go 10 mi. (half unpaved), pass Lower Blue Lake on east shore, drive through campground to trailhead parking at south end of Upper Blue Lake. At 8100 ft.

Map: Markleeville

H: Granite Lake, 4 mi., 800 ft.; Grouse Lake, 10 mi., 2200 ft.; Devils Corral loop, 9.5 mi. (5 mi. off-trail), 1600 ft.

The **Granite Lake** trail immediately crosses a stream between the two Blue Lakes, then climbs easily through pleasing forest. Granite Lake is set among yellow-granite formations, which make for good side-scrambles. To **Grouse Lake**, the trail leaves westerly from Granite's south shore, hooking south and then west again and climbing through confused topography—it's easy to go astray. Grouse Lake is tucked away among aspen and mixed conifers.

To get to **Devils Corral loop**, home to a wildflower extravaganza and some towering western white pine, follow the road/trail north and up the east shore of Upper Blue Lake. You'll go through a forest of huge red firs and then down to join up with the Summit City Creek trail. Walk 2 miles down the trail and look south into a box canyon: that's Devils Corral. If you reach the confluence of Devils Corral and Summit City creeks, you've gone too far. Cross the water and walk south and up through Devils Corral—now off-trail. To return, go up and out the lowest saddle to the southeast. From the forested saddle, you'll see Upper Blue Lake, and the route back.

BP: Grouse Lake and it's environs, with lakelets and maze-like topography, provide hidden backpack getaways, even on busy weekends. *Local lore:* Just south of here is where legendary recluse Monty Wolf stayed lost for years.

MB: Expect people on summer weekends, but mountain bikers can ride from Lower Blue Lakes to Lost Lakes, northeast of Upper Blue, or up the Forestdale Divide, which is north of Upper Blue. Also see TH17 and TH16 mountain bike notes.

B: Canoeing and kayaking in Blue Lakes affords good mountain views, although the lake's water level is often low, revealing dirt and a few stumps. Twin Lake is a woodsy choice for paddlers.

F: Boat trolling and shore casting for trout in **Upper Blue Lake**. The beaver ponds at **Lost Lakes**, a short distance from Upper Blue, support large numbers of good-sized brook trout. Walk into **Granite Lake** to fly-cast for cutthroat.

19.   WET MEADOWS   H, BP, MB, F

Best for: Hidden Sierran valley, thrilling peak and crest views, wildflowers, biking and horsing around lakes.

Park: Take Blue Lakes Road, 3 mi. west of Picketts Jct. At 9 mi. in (after 4 mi. unpaved) take left fork toward Sunset Lakes and Wet Meadows. After 2.5 mi., take right fork to Indian Valley. For Indian Valley hikes, park in open area after .5-mile. For Raymond and Pleasant Valley, continue for 1 mi., around east shore of lakes, and park at trailhead. At 7900 feet. Car-shuttle, park second car in Pleasant Valley, TH29.

Map: Markleeville

H: Raymond Lake, 12 mi., 1200 ft.; Raymond Peak, 14 mi. (2 mi. off-trail), 2200 ft.; Indian Valley, 6 mi., 500 ft.; Reynolds Peak, 11 mi. (5 mi. off-trail), 1700 ft.; Pleasant Valley car-shuttle, 7.5 miles, minus 2000 ft.

The trail to **Raymond Lake** picks up the PCT southbound, beginning at the backside, or west, of its saw-tooth, volcanic ridge. The trail wiggles a contour all the way around to approach from the east. Raymond Lake is in a cirque below the peak. To reach **Raymond Peak** from the lake, go around the left, east, as you face the water, off-trail, up that shoulder. Except for possible snow, it's easy but steep going until you get to the peculiar rocks at the top. You'll have to use hands as you make your way the last bit up Ray's spires, but it's not a hard climb. *Watch out:* Approaching Raymond Lake or Peak from the west is tempting but not advised. It becomes steep and craggy. Also, stay on trails in the Wet Meadows basin; it holds 6 or 7 small lakes, creeks that run parallel in opposite directions and has no great vantage points—all this spells l-o-s-t.

For the **Pleasant Valley car-shuttle**, a trail forks off and down from the Raymond Lake trail, just as you get out of the initial forested area and pick up views. Manzanita is an issue if going off-trail on this trip. To hike **Indian Valley**, with its pockets of wildflowers and panorama of the backside of Raymond and Reynolds peaks, walk the road south. It becomes just a trail after 1.5 miles, climbing gradually to a low ridge that overlooks the Ebbetts Pass area. The vantage point is among large junipers and other conifers. To do **Reynolds Peak**, go off-trail at this Ebbetts overlook, bearing west along the flat, open ridge for 2 miles, and then dipping through a saddle. After the saddle, you make a 1200-foot scramble up Reynolds' southeast shoulder—the very top is a spire, difficult to climb.

BP: Raymond Lake has 4 or 5 campsites—2 or 3 prime. On summer weekends you'll have company. Don't plan on fires, since fuel is scarce, and prepare for wind. Notwithstanding all that, Raymond Lake is highly recommended. Indian Valley is seldom used by backpackers and has some great spots, especially for packers with a collapsible water container who can camp further from water sources.

MB: You can park where pavement ends in Charity Valley, ride 4 miles to Wet Meadows road, and then ride a forested, 7-mile circuit among 5 lakes, named in fishing notes below.

F: **Tamarack, Upper and Lower Sunset, Summit and Wet Meadows lakes,** all accessible by road, have brook and cutthroat trout. Early season fly-fishing and boat fishing later on. Hike into **Raymond Lake** for golden trout—which you may wish to catch-and-release since this is a rare species and popular spot.

20. HOPE VALLEY   H, CC, F

Best for:	Picnics, fall color, photography, taking a plunge in the river, moonlight skis, children and grandparent walks—just being there.
Parking:	Three choices: (a) At turnout on Hwy. 88/89, immediately east of Picketts Junction. (b) At turnout on Hwy. 88, .25-mi. west of Picketts. (c) Where West Carson River crosses under Hwy. 88, 1 mi. west of Picketts. At 7000 ft.
Map:	Freel Peak

H: Three short walks, up to 4 mi., no elevation.

Hope Valley, with its pastoral majesty, cannot be described without hyperbole. From **parking spot "a,"** walk .25-mile across the often-wet meadow to the confluence of the West Carson River and two creeks, a place to let the dog swim or to enjoy a book or a bottle of wine. At **spot "b"** an old wagon road meanders through the heart of the valley, 1.5 miles north toward Luther Pass. At **spot "c"** you can walk an abandoned road upriver, a few miles if you wish, passing many spots for picnics, reflection or swimming. About .5-mile in, look for **Roger's Rock**, a granite tabletop from which to take a plunge.

CC: Moonlight skiing at spots "b" and "c" is excellent. Often, the surface freezes to a crust, and Nordic skiers can skate a vast, sparkling snow field.

F: The **West Carson River** runs from upper Hope Valley to Woodfords, mostly accessible by car. River habitat ranges from free-flowing water and pools in Hope Valley to white water in Woodfords Canyon. You'll find four species of trout: cutthroat, rainbow, brown and brook.

Forestdale Divide

21. BURNSIDE LAKE H, MB, CC, B, F

Best for: Big-feeling hike without much effort, reaching Alpine's most-recognizable historic peak, resting at small cascade, wildflower meadow.

Park: Take Burnside Lake Road (unpaved), due south at Picketts Jct., Hwy. 88/89. Drive in 6 mi. to Burnside Lake. At 8100 ft. For car-shuttle, park second car at Grover State Park, TH31.

Map: Freel Peak and Markleeville

H: Hot Springs Valley overlook, 2.5 mi., no elevation; Grover car-shuttle, 4.5 mi., minus 2100 ft.; Hawkins Peak, 6 mi., (3 mi. off-trail), 2000 ft.

To **Hot Springs Valley overlook**, take the trail southeast from Burnside Lake—on the east side of the willow-fringed meadow just south of the lake. Beyond the far end of the meadowland, following the creek out, you'll come to an overlook where benches of yellow granite afford views of the valley. Note a small cascade and pool below the trail. Also, the sculpted granite upward from the east side of the trail is an interesting side jaunt for non-car-shuttle hikers. This is the ridge most visible from the hot pool at the park.

To **Grover Hot Springs car-shuttle**, take the switchbacks on down from the overlook area, through cedar and pine forests. To reach **Hawkins Peak**, beginning at Burnside Lake, go off-trail, north-northeast from the middle of the lake. Stay east of the mine road, which is .75 miles away from Burnside. After about 1000 feet of upping, you'll come to the open slopes of Hawkins, sporting dwarf sage and mule ears, with a clear view of the peak's knobbed top. A road gets you across an intervening swale. The last few hundred feet is up talus, before reaching the tabletop. *Local lore:* Near the top, look for a rock inscripted by Harry Hawkins, one of Alpine's pioneers whose ranch house still stands on the east side of Hwy. 89, one mile south of Woodfords—on private property.

Watch out: If lightening is anywhere in the area, do not attempt Hawkins Peak.

MB: Park at south side of Picketts Junction. Ride 6 mi. in to Burnside Lake. The road presents a number of options, including branches east toward Pickett Peak or slopes of Hawkins Peak. You can also go toward Sorensen's Resort or west into Hope Valley.

CC: Park at Picketts Junction. Forested Burnside Lake Road has reliable snow, with some good downhill runs on the road itself, and off-trail options toward Hawkins Peak and into Hope Valley.

B: Kayaking and canoeing on Burnside Lake with forested shores and rock views.

F: Drive to **Burnside Lake** to tube for shore cast or rainbows and brookies.

22. SORENSEN'S CLIFFS H, MB, CC

Best for: Fall colors, Hope Valley views, Carson River cascade.
Park: .75-mi. east of Picketts Jct. On Hwy. 88/89, spaces on either side of highway, just west of Sorensen's Resort. At 7000 ft. For cascade, park at Hope Valley Resort, 1 mi. east of Picketts.
Map: Freel Peak

H: Sorensen's Cliffs, 3.5 mi., 1000 ft.; Pickett Peak, 8 mi. (3 mi. off-trail), 2100 ft.; West Carson Cascade, .5 mi., 200 ft.

To **Sorensen's Cliffs,** take the gated road up from the highway as it switchbacks through mixed conifers, aspen and willow groves. The volcanic cliffs overlook Hope Valley and Woodfords Canyon.

To get to **Pickett Peak**, Hawkins' neighbor, continue on the road, until the point at which it starts to lose elevation. At that point go off-trail up the peak's northwest shoulder. *Watch out:* The talus and boulders which comprise Pickett Peak will be a problem to dogs and people not comfortable with bouldering. *Note:* You can also reach Pickett Peak with less elevation gain by taking Burnside Lake Road, TH 21, and then turning left, east, on Forest Service 053—until reaching the point below the northwest shoulder of the peak.

The **West Carson Cascade** is visible from Hwy. 88 and accessible by taking the short walk through the Hope Valley Resort campground, and bouldering up a few feet from the bridge at the river.

MB: This uphill pump connects up with the Burnside Lake system of roads.
CC: Marked trails from here connect up with Burnside Lake Road and Hope Valley. Check with Hope Valley Outdoor Center and Sorensen's for info and rentals.

23. HORSETHIEF CANYON H, BP, F

Best for: Getting a high-country experience early in the season, pockets of tall wildflowers, cowboy relics, falling water.
Park: 4 mi. west of Woodfords on Hwy. 88/89. Across from Snowshoe Springs Campground. At 6600 ft.
Map: Freel Peak

H: Horsethief Canyon, 4 mi., 1300 ft.; Careys Peak, 8 mi. (4 mi. off-trail), 2200 ft.

Horsethief Canyon trail begins steeply, making switchbacks through granite sand and then skirting a white-water stream below volcanic buttresses. Water thunders by. At the top are large junipers which lead the way to sloping meadows. Continue straight across a Forest Service road, following a trail that features lush wildflowers in midsummer, especially at the upper end of the meadows.

To **Careys Peak**, turn eastward, off-trail, after crossing the Forest Service road at the top of the canyon. Continue for one mile, climbing and hooking south, making sure not to get suckered into Hidden Canyon, which is between Horsethief and the shoulder of Careys Peak. Final approach to the peak is up its northern shoulder, with brush and boulders to deal with for a short stretch. Careys Peak overlooks Woodfords and is the source of the Washo sacred falls.

Local Lore: In the 1850s, horse thieves preying on California emigrants would bring stolen stock up this canyon and loop eastward back into the Carson Valley, where they would sell the fattened animals back to other emigrants. You may well come upon remnants of cowboy corrals and cabins.

BP: Horsethief Canyon is best for one-night pack trips, good for kids who can do the initial upping.

F: Walk in 1.5 miles to **Horsethief Creek** at top of canyon to fly-cast for brookies.

24. WILLOW CREEK H, MB, CC, F

Best for: Group hikes with view of Hope Valley and Sierran Crest, fall color, biking and skiing.

Park: At gate .5-mi. north of Picketts Jct. on Hwy. 89. At 7000 ft. For Horsethief car-shuttle, park second car at TH23.

Map: Freel Peak

H: Hope Valley view, 5 mi., 1000 ft.; Horsethief car-shuttle, 6.5 mi., 1500 ft.

The **Willow Creek** trail—Forest Service 025, gated— begins gently along the creek through mostly lodgepole pine. Then begins a series of long, gradual switchbacks, topping out at a forested ridge with spot-on views. Wildflower pockets also will be found at several ephemeral drainages up higher.

For the **Horsethief car-shuttle**, continue on the road across an intervening level zone before descending into upper Horsethief Canyon meadows via switchbacks. Early in the summer, at the saddle on the road itself, notice the pine cone seeds sprouting young Jeffreys and lodgepole.

MB: To do the loop, you will have to walk your bike the last fraction of a mile down the Horsethief Canyon trail, and then ride Hwy 89 back to the Willow Creek parking area. Good riding surface, other than that. You can also explore other roads which take off toward Horse Meadow, TH25.

CC: Moonlight skiing is good here at the lower part of the road, as well as the more open area of Hope Valley across the highway from the trailhead parking. Good downhill for beginning and intermediate skiers as you continue on the road.

F: Use this trailhead to fish **Willow Creek** and the **West Carson River** before it falls into Woodfords Canyon.

25. HORSE MEADOW H, MB, CC

Best for:	Peaks with Tahoe and high desert views, downhill run through granite sand, mountain biking and horseback riding, old-growth juniper forest.
Park:	Drive about 1.5 mi. toward Tahoe from Picketts Jct. on Hwy. 89, .25-mi. past the old barn on big bend. Turn on dirt road, Forest Service 051. Go in 6 mi. and park at Horse Meadow. At 8400 ft.
Map:	Freel Peak

H: Fountain Place, 6 mi., 900 ft.; Jobs Peak, 6 mi., 2200 ft.; Jobs Sister, 5 mi., 2400 ft.; Freel Peak, 6 mi., 2500 ft. *Note:* You will find trail segments at higher elevations on these peak hikes, but overall about half the walking distances are off-trail.

The trail to **Fountain Place** via Armstrong Pass takes off to the left, or north, at the bridge on the western end of Horse Meadow. Fountain Place is the confluence of two creeks below Freel Peak that forms Trout Creek, a major tributary of Tahoe. This trail continues to Tahoe. To reach **all three peaks**, take a right-bearing road at upper Horse Meadow and drive to the end. Proceeding off-trail right from the get-go, climb steeply, keeping the drainage on your left, up and up. You top-out above the larger conifers and contour easterly and to your left. Aim for the saddle between Jobs and Jobs Sister.

To **Jobs Peak** from the saddle—which would be one, yahoo ski run down to the Carson Valley—a trail takes off southeasterly. For **Jobs Sister**—and her views of Tahoe and the valley—take the same approach as Jobs, but cross the saddle to the northwest, and make switchbacks through granite formations to the top.

For **Freel Peak**, walk across a 1.5-mile saddle that connects Freel with Jobs Sister. After passing through granite sand and dwarf whitebark southwest of Jobs Sister, and a sandy hogback also in between the two peaks, take a trail to the top. From Freel, drop off due south through hundreds of feet of sandy descent, down to the middle of Horse Meadow. Cross the stream and find the road back up to the car. **To do Freel Peak without Jobs Sister**, park just after the bridge at Fountain Place road, and approach Freel directly from its south— making switchbacks at will, as your legs and lungs dictate.

Watch out: From the top of any of these peaks, get a bearing on where you parked your car. Three streams converge in Horse Meadow, making micro navigating hard after you've descended.

MB: Park at the gate at Hwy. 89 for a 12-mile ride up to Horse Meadow, with options to take spur roads that join with Forest Service 025 and drop into Hope Valley at Willow Creek, TH24, or into Horsethief Canyon, TH23.

CC: Great for larger groups of intermediate skiers, with steeper runs optional for those who go off road. A sleeper area.

26. TAHOE RIM TRAIL AT LUTHER PASS H, CC

Best for: Out-of-the-way day hike, old-growth conifers and lush wildflowers, seldom-scaled, but famous peak with Hope Valley views.

Park: On Hwy. 89, 3 mi. toward Tahoe from Picketts Jct., just north of Luther Pass. Look for trailhead sign. At 7700 ft.

Map: Freel Peak

H: Tahoe Rim view, 6 mi., 1300 ft.; Thompson Peak, 8 mi. (4 mi. off-trail), 1400 ft.

Tahoe Rim Trail, only recently completed, circles the lake; this is one of its many trailheads. After about 3 miles on the trail, you can climb off-trail to the north for a look toward Tahoe. The trail continues into Fountain Place, which is also reachable from Horse Meadow, TH25.

To get to **Thompson Peak** leave the trail after about 2 miles, hooking to the east through **Freel Meadows** and its tall flowers. After about a mile, turn to the south, walking the gradual shoulder to the tree-topped peak. From the trailhead, you will have circled up and behind the Thompson Peak. Named for Snowshoe Thompson, this is not the highest peak around, but it gives you a good look at Hope Valley and the Sierran Crest.

CC: Popular skiing is across the highway from the trailhead, at Grass Lake, which is a Sno-Park (permit required, available at Sorensen's). The best ski, however, may be at the Luther Pass turnout, where a road leads out the south side of the parking area, making a good run into Hope Valley; this area is not a Sno-Park.

Autumn Aspen

27. BIG MEADOW H, BP, MB, F

Best for: Old-growth red fir forest, first-class camping lakes with wildflowers on the way.

Park: Look for improved trailhead parking lot on Hwy. 89, 3 mi. north of Luther Pass. At 7200 ft.

Maps: Fallen Leaf and Freel Peak.

H: Big Meadow, 2 mi., 700 ft.; Dardanelles Lake, 7 mi., 1200 ft.; Round Lake, 6.5 mi., 1000 ft.

Coming up a north-facing, steep trail for the first mile or so, you may encounter snow in early summer on the way to **Big Meadow**. Big Meadow features fairly good wildflowers, and its creek, which can be deep but not dangerous to cross, makes a good lunch spot.

To **Dardanelles Lake**, you head south, climbing gradually out of Big Meadow. Then take a right, west, fork on the trail, which will contour around to a hillside of huge red fir. From a trail junction at that point, the trail to Dardanelles Lake drops into the drainage of the Upper Truckee. Dardanelles, with its complex shoreline of granite and pools, is a pleasing backpack destination and swimming lake.

To get to **Round Lake**, continue contouring along the red fir slope—not taking the trail across the drainage—climbing and dipping through a zone of hidden lakelets and rumpled topography. Towering above Round Lake is an enormous "buffalo head" outcropping, a feature which can be seen from many points in this area.

BP: A popular summer trailhead; expect company on weekends at Dardanelles and Round lakes.

MB: Mr. Toad's Wild Ride, a tough downhill run of 12 miles to Meyers, begins by heading northeast to Tucker Flat on the Tahoe Rim Trail. Follow the northwest, left, trail fork down the Saxon Creek drainage, and keep taking left-fork options on roads as you get closer to Meyers. Bikers can also take an easier route down from Big Meadow. An unpaved road leads down to Christmas Valley, and then follows the Upper Truckee River along a road through houses, popping out at Meyers.

F: Day hike or backpack to **Round Lake**—stock varies.

Markleeville

Webster School

Markleeville didn't become the county seat for Alpine's first 11 years, not until Silver Mountain City on Ebbetts Pass went bust in 1875. During those Silver-boom years, the regional population was a transient 25,000—more than five-times that of Los Angeles—with miners and entrepreneurs roaming six mining districts. Today, Alpine's population is about 1,000, by far the smallest among California counties. Agriculture was the county's mainstay for most of this century, and many family holdings operating today date back to pioneer days. But remnants of other, bygone homesteads dot this region; ranchers, farmers and sawyers who kept the mines supplied and were gone when it was over.

In recent years, Markleeville's mountains and rivers and meadows have become the silver mine, as recreational tourism has become the primary economic force. Scenic resources are complemented by ranching families who to date have withstood pressures to develop private holdings adjacent to public lands. Local groups, such as Friends of Hope Valley and Alpine Scenic Alliance, as well as individuals, work to maintain Alpine's natural resources.

East and north of Markleeville are piñon forests and sage lands with volcanic outcroppings, the historic wintering grounds of the Washo Indians. The Washo—whose ancestors 8,000 years ago blazed trails that exist today—were hunters and gatherers. They harvested some 12,000 plants and animals from the wild gardens of the Sierra. Washo baskets are known as the finest in the world, and those woven by Dat-So-La-Lee are coveted museum pieces. Other than baskets, obsidian arrowheads and grinding rocks, found throughout the region, are the only physical reminders of the ancient Washo nation.

Washo lands are cleaved by the East Carson River, running through a canyon leading to Nevada. The East Carson Canyon was the route taken by Jedediah Smith and other trappers, the first white men in California in the late 1820s. It was also the passage for the Expedition of the Western Territories by General John Fremont. Led by Kit Carson in the early 1840s, this was first recorded passage through the Sierra.

The upstream drainage of the East Carson River—Hot Springs Valley, Pleasant Valley, Wolf Creek, Silver King and Bagley Valleys—is ideal for all kinds of Alpine recreational pursuits. Saw-toothed Raymond Peak and humongous Silver Peak, landmarks visible due south from Reno, are just two mountains hanging above town.

Ebbetts Pass, with Scossa Cow Camp the Silver Mountain City ruins nearby, was once planned as the first railroad route through the Sierra, but its engineer suffered an untimely death by drowning. Now the Pacific Crest Trail is the major route. West of Ebbetts, the Mokelumne River flows to the San Joaquin and the San Francisco Bay. East of the pass, Silver Creek and many other streams, feed the East Carson River, headed for the Carson Sink in the Great Basin.

Monitor Pass was completed in 1954, the last pass engineered in California. On top of Monitor are the broad shoulders of Leviathan Peak, with its sage, pine and aspen expanses. Basque sheepherders have left many artful carvings in the hinterlands of this region. The westward view is of the Sierra Nevada, an ocean of peaks, and to the east are the sublime Slinkard and Antelope valleys, with the Sweetwater Mountains a short hop south.

Although not much commerce travels Monitor, almost all camel traffic in the Sierra took this route. Camels were coaxed through Monitor in the late 1800s, on the last leg of a long journey from their middle-Eastern homelands and headed to haul salt in the Lahontan area of Nevada. The animals balked at the cliffs, but when the first one was pulled along the rest followed—down "Dump Canyon," which leads from south of Monitor's Company Meadows into to Slinkard Valley.

Raymond Lake and Peak

JIM DUNN

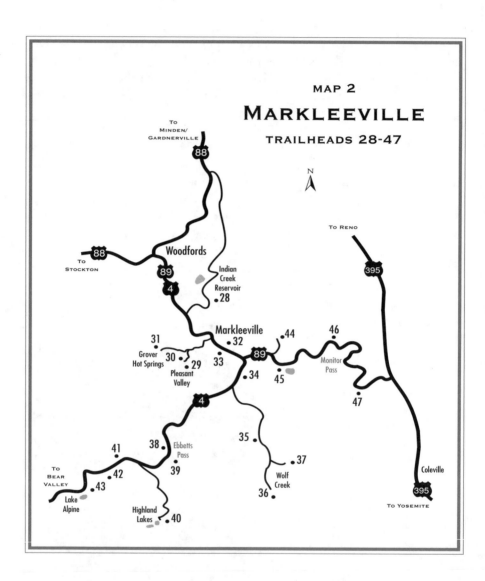

MAP 2

MARKLEEVILLE

TRAILHEADS 28-47

N

To
Minden/
Gardnerville

88

To Reno

88

To
Stockton

Woodfords

89

4

Indian
Creek
Reservoir

28

395

Markleeville

31

32

44

46

Grover
Hot Springs

30

29

33

89

Monitor
Pass

Pleasant
Valley

34

45

47

4

35

41

38

Ebbetts
Pass

37

To
Bear
Valley

42

39

Coleville

43

Wolf
Creek

395

Lake
Alpine

36

To Yosemite

Highland
Lakes

40

TRAILHEADS 28–47
MAP 2

H=DAY HIKING, BP=BACKPACKING, MB=MOUNTAIN BIKING,
CC=CROSS COUNTRY SKIING, B=BOATING, F=FISHING

28. CURTZ LAKE/INDIAN CREEK H, MB, CC, B, F

Best for:	Spring or fall exploring of Washo country, early season flowers, bald eagle sightings, horseback or mountain bike rides.
Park:	Turn on Airport Road off Hwy. 89/4, midway between Woodfords and Markleeville. Hikers park at Curtz Lake, 2.5 mi. in. At 6200 ft. For Markleeville car-shuttle, park second car in Markleeville. For Indian Creek car-shuttle and Stevens Lake, park second car at Indian Creek Reservoir, 3 mi. from Curtz Lake on Airport Rd.
Maps:	Markleeville and Freel Peak

H: Summit Lake, 2.5 mi., 200 ft.; Summit Lake to Indian Creek car-shuttle, 4.5 mi., elevation loss. Fremonts Crossing, 4 mi., 1000 ft., Fremonts Crossing to Markleeville car-shuttle, 4.5 mi. (2.5 mi. off-trail), 300 ft.; Stevens Lake, .5-mi., no elevation.

To **Summit Lake**, take the trail which begins at the gate on the north side of Curtz Lake. Keep an eye out for eagles, hawks as well as waterfowl on the way to this small but pleasant lake. To **Indian Creek car-shuttle** take the trail out the northeast side of Summit Lake, through an intervening flat, and then east and down through piñon forest. To **Stevens Lake**, drive to Indian Creek Reservoir and take the short walk from the far end of the campground.

The trail to **Fremonts Crossing** is on the opposite side of the road, east side, from Curtz Lake. It takes you 2 miles down to the East Carson River Canyon, where Fremont's expedition passed through in 1844. Today during the early part of the summer you might see rafters shooting by this stretch of the river. For **Markleeville car-shuttle,** head upriver from the crossing, off-trail, scrambling and side-hilling outcroppings for the first mile. Then you walk through Jeffrey pine forests that border the pastures leading to the town.

Note: A nature trail begins at the south end of Curtz Lake, across the highway. And you can extend this short nature walk by going off-trail from the southerly loop of the trail. Head up, southerly, to volcanic nubs with dead-on views of Raymond and other peaks above Markleeville.

MB: BLM roads take off from Indian Creek Reservoir, on its east side. These roads connect with Diamond Valley Road, which can be ridden west toward Woodfords and then back to the car via Highway 89/4, making about a 10-mile loop.

CC: After or during big storms, Airport Road to Indian Creek is a good Nordic choice. Steven's Lake is often frozen in midwinter and can be used as a rink for ski-skating. This should only be attempted during the coldest weather, as breaking ice is extremely dangerous.

B: Indian Creek is large enough for sailing, and also a convenient spot to make a kayak or canoe excursion.

F: Walk in to **Summit Lake** to float tube for brook trout, or drive to **Indian Creek Reservoir** for some of the area's biggest rainbows, brooks and Lahontan cut throat. Boat ramp available.

29. PLEASANT VALLEY H, BP, MB, CC, F

Best for: Fall color, early-season flowers, classic Alpine valley, picnicking, swimming holes, horseback riding, short hikes, second-car trailhead for shuttle hikes.

Park: Take Pleasant Valley Road, 1.5 mi. west of Markleeville on Hot Springs Road. Keep right, uphill past homes, 3 mi. (2 mi. unpaved) into Pleasant Valley to end of road. At 6000 ft.

Map: Markleeville

H: Pleasant Valley trail, 2 to 7 mi., 100 to 800 ft. Trail continues to Wet Meadows, TH19.

Pleasant Valley, with Raymond Peak looking down upon cottonwoods and mixed conifers fed by a many-pooled stream, is a great place for both dawdling and serious hiking. Along the creek are sandy beaches for wading and swimming. Energetic hikers can continue on the trail as it gains elevation after about 2 miles, crossing the fanned-out drainage on its way up to Wet Meadows and Raymond Peak. *Note:* Some of Pleasant Valley is private property; heed signs.

If you don't cross the drainage, and continue up the northwest sector or the valley, a hidden falls lies just off-trail, about two miles up from the creek crossing. The trail peters out—stay lower to avoid manzanita, walking up granite faces in a few places. Several trail-side perches afford misted looks at white-water shooting through a narrow section of the bedrock.

Local lore: History buffs might try **Raymond Canyon** midway on the south side of Pleasant Valley—locals tell of miner's goodies stashed away in a cave that were left one winter and not retrieved in the spring.

BP: Pleasant Valley is a good trailhead to end a Raymond Lake backpack. Pacific Crest Trail trekkers also drop down here to resupply.

MB: Park at end of paved road and ride in a couple miles to enjoy the creek.

CC: Ski in and down the 2 miles at the end of the road and then west into the valley. A very good area, when snowpack is adequate.

F: **Pleasant Valley Creek** is a renowned catch-and-release spot. Fly-fishing only with single barbless hook. Limits posted and enforced. Rainbows and browns.

30. THORNBURG CANYON H, MB

Best for:	Pleasant Valley view, getting away from crowds, interesting cliffs.
Park:	Turn on Pleasant Valley Road, 2 mi. east of Markleeville on Hot Springs Road. Go about .25-mile, veer right on dirt road, pass homes on left, and continue 3 mi. until county road ends. At 6300 ft. *Note:* The road crosses two creeks, pesky in early spring and summer, when 4-wheel is required. High clearance always recommended.
Map:	Markleeville

H: Thornburg Canyon, 9 mi., 1800 ft.

Thornburg Canyon trail rises out of a lush forest of Jeffrey pine and aspen, and into an open, manzanita and granite sand area. A few hundred feet to the south of this spot is a Pleasant Valley overlook. Then rejoin the trail as it jogs north and climbs steeply in the shade of alder and mixed conifers, alongside Spratt Creek. *Note*: Due to shade, snow may linger in the middle section of this hike.

The top of Thornburg Canyon, which is a rugged zone between Jeff Davis and Markleeville peaks, offers off-trail scrambling to spires with commanding views. As the crow flies, Grover Hot Springs is a short distance from here; but the intervening country is extremely rough and complex.

MB: Park at Pleasant Valley Road for a 10 mile round-trip ride to the overlook described in the hike.

31. GROVER HOT SPRINGS H, CC, F

Best for: Soak and walk to falls, classic Alpine valley, pockets of wildflowers, dipping in creek.
Park: At Grover State Park, 4 mi. west of Markleeville on Hot Springs Road. Day use fee. Additional parking at pool. At 5900 ft.
Map: Markleeville

H: Grover Falls, 4 mi., 800 ft.

The main **Grover Falls** trail is on the north side of the meadow, through Jeffrey pine and the region's best cedar grove. It's a flat stroll along the creek for a mile, and then up through granite benches to the falls—which are more a cataract. Another trail leads back to the park on the south side of the creek, ending up at the hot pool. Pockets of some of Alpine's best wildflowers are tucked away around Grover.

Note: Two trails lead out of Hot Springs Valley, one to Burnside Lake, TH21, and another to Charity Valley, TH16. See those trailhead descriptions.

CC: Hot Springs Valley is leisurely forest skiing, with some uphill excursions possible on the slopes opposite the pool. Fallen trees and a number of brooks make for hassles when snowpack is insufficient.
F: **Markleeville Creek**, which runs along Hot Springs Road, has a number of fishing holes for fly-casters looking mostly for rainbows. Six or seven creeks— with headwaters in Hot Springs Valley, Thornburg Canyon and Pleasant Valley— all come together by the time they reach Markleeville Creek just west of town. This creek, which used to be called the Middle Fork of the Carson River, joins the East Carson a mile downstream from Markleeville. All of which is to say, fly-fishermen have plenty to explore.

32. HANGMANS BRIDGE H, MB, CC, B, F

Best for: Early- and late-season hiking, adventuring in piñon forests of Washo country, low-elevation flowers, biking.
Park: At Hangmans Bridge, 1.5 mi. south of Markleeville on Hwy. 89/4. Parking area immediately south of bridge. At 5500 ft.
Maps: Markleeville and Topaz Lake

H: Carson Confluence, 3 mi., 200 ft.; Barney Riley Jeep Trail/East Carson Canyon loop 6 to 10 mi. (2 or 3 mi. off-trail), 900 ft.

Grover Hot Springs

To reach the **Carson Confluence**, where the East Carson River meets Markleeville Creek, take the road leading from the gate and keep left. You can extend this walk by continuing on abandoned roads downriver through the canyon another couple miles. *Note:* Portions along the river are private property; heed signs.

The **Barney Riley Jeep Trail** takes off to the right, uphill, about .25-mile from the parking area. It ascends to an open, often-sunny ridge with vistas of a wave of Sierran peaks to the west. BRJT continues over hill and dale into Nevada. You'll want to pick a spot at the top, near where the trail contours eastward from the river canyon for the last time, and go down off-trail to the river. At the bottom, find the old road and head upriver to the trailhead.

Watch out: Avoid a couple precipitous escarpments by staying mainly in the creases of the slope rather than coming down its shoulders.

MB: The BRJT also connects with roads leading to Haypress Flat and the Leviathan Mine roads, which are accessed from Hwy. 89 below Monitor Pass—see TH44 and TH46. Near the trailhead, clay soil can make for sticky going in the spring.

CC: The BRJT is a good choice after a winter storm that dumps in Markleeville. Due to southern exposure and arid locale, snow is unreliable.

B: Hangmans Bridge is a renowned put-in for rafters. The East Carson Canyon has hot springs, cliffs and mixed conifer forests. Takeout for this overnight or day trip is before the dam off Hwy. 395 south of Gardnerville. Kayakers and adventurous rafters put in at several spots upriver from Hangmans, making for more exhilarating runs and less hassle with the car-shuttle. Several white-water chutes can be spotted from the highway along the upper section—tailor made for kayakers by the flood of 1998. A number of outfitters service this river.

F: You can walk down the **East Carson River**, fly-casting for browns and rainbows. This downriver section is a California Department of Fish and Game Wild Trout area, with special restrictions. To fish upriver, drive Hwy. 89/4, looking for turnouts and spur roads along a stretch that extends beyond the turnoff to Wolf Creek Road, on Highway 4. Rainbows and browns are the most common trout caught here.

33. POOR BOY CANYON H, MB, CC

Best for: Exploring out-of-the-way places, views, looking for bears and wildlife, early-season wildflowers.

Park: Take Poor Boy Canyon Road, .75 mi. south of Markleeville on Hwy. 89/4. At 5700 ft.

Map: Markleeville

H: Silver Mountain City overlook, 12 mi., 1900 ft. Shorter and longer hikes, depending on where you choose to park.

Hikers may wish to drive in a few miles on **Poor Boy Canyon Road,** following Forest Service Road 040, to end of the county road. About six miles from that point, you will come to the top, giving you views of Silver Mountain City and Silver Peak to the south, Raymond Peak to the west, and the Crystal Range of Tahoe to the north. Poor Boy Canyon is a likely place to see wildlife, including bear, since it is less-frequently used than other trailheads.

Note: Some of Poor Boy is private property; heed signs.

Local Lore: Off-trail exploring may lead to old mines and artifacts, as this area borders several historic mining districts. Remains of a historic trail can be found walking up the drainage of Poor Boy Canyon.

MB: Although clay soil can be nasty at times, Poor Boy Canyon is a very large and interesting area for mountain bikers, with several Forest Service roads. Be mindful of getting suckered into logging spur roads or skid trails.

CC: Snow is unreliable, but during heavy storm years, or after a storm, Poor Boy Canyon Road has plenty of elevation and open tracts for Nordic trips. A good midwinter choice, if snow is on the ground in Markleeville.

34. SILVER HILL H, MB

> **Best for:**   Out-of-the-way hike through old mining district, horseback or bike the high country.
> **Park:**   At Silver Hill Road on Hwy. 4, 1 mi. south of jct. with Hwy. 89. At 5700 ft. For car-shuttle, park second car at Heenan Lake, TH45.
> **Map:**   Topaz Lake

H: Silver Hill, 7 mi. (2.5 mi. off-trail), 1800 ft.; Bagley Valley car-shuttle, 8.5 mi. (3.5 mi. off-trail), 2000 ft.

To **Silver Hill,** a landmark for one of Alpine's historic mining districts, take the road as it climbs and twists, passing two cabins—private mining claims—near the top. At the end of the road, turn off-trail due south to Silver Hill, which, at 7500 feet, is not the highest point around. An unnamed peak of 8031 feet lies a mile to its northeast.

To drop into **Bagley Valley** for the car-shuttle, head east, off-trail, from the north side of Silver Hill, cutting between the saddle of the unnamed peak and its 7956-foot neighbor to the southeast. From that saddle, make the steep downing, due east, until you reach the road out along the west shore of Heenan Lake.

MB: Silver Hill is a leg-burner for cyclists. And riding the steep slope all the way into Bagley Valley is not possible for a sane person. Mountain bikers can, however, escort their bikes down the steepest part to Bagley, as per hiking description, and take the road out to pavement. From Heenan Lake, loop back via the highways to the Silver Hill trailhead.

35. SILVER PEAK H

Best for:	Mondo hike through wild country to top of a major Sierran peak.
Park:	Take Wolf Creek Road, off Hwy 4, 3 mi. south of jct. of Hwys. 89/4. Go several miles as road becomes unpaved and climbs a washboard surface. At the top, before the road drops into Wolf Creek—and .25-mile past the rock quarry—take the Forest Service Road that veers off to the right (4-wheel only, but not difficult). Go about 1.5 mi. until road forks and park. At 7200 ft. If you don't want to drive in this last road, plan on another 3 mi. and 800 ft.
Maps:	Topaz Lake and Markleeville

H: Silver Peak, 12 mi. (all off-trail), 3500 ft.

Silver Peak at 10,800 feet is a tough hike and should be attempted only by fit, experienced hikers who can read a topo map. On the other hand, it is doable and delivers an out-there, big-time High Sierra experience. From the trailhead, take the north-heading branch of a road into an old logging landing, about .5-mile. Then turn west and climb steeply through trees. You'll pop out into an open area, with scree slopes. Keep climbing with a general bearing of southwest, up a shoulder between scree and brush—this is the most problematic section of the hike. Also be wary of going up false peaks, as you are still several miles from Silver Peak at this stage.

After this initial scramble, you'll recognize the shoulder you can observe from the Carson Valley, heading west/southwest from you. The Dixon Creek drainage will be far below on your left. A high meadow, with an ephemeral stream, is a good resting spot before making your away up and around an intervening craggy ridge that stands between you and the final, 800-foot climb to Silver Peak. *Watch out:* Leave early, carry water. On certain years, or late in the season, you'll find little water on this hike.

Note: Before driving to the trailhead, you may wish to get the big picture by driving Hwy. 88 into the Carson Valley, north of Woodfords. From there, look south. The double-headed mountain that lines up with the north-south highway is Silver, and the shoulder you see as its horizon from left to right is the route of ascent.

36. WOLF CREEK SOUTH H, BP, F

Best for: Fall color, wildflowers, horseback riding, variety of trees, peaks overlooking creek canyon—the best of mid-elevation Alpine hiking, backpack options.

Park: Take Wolf Creek Road, 3 mi. south of jct. Hwys. 89/4. Road unpaved after 2 mi., but two-wheelable. Continue south in Wolf Creek Meadow, 2.5 mi. and park at trailhead parking. At 6200 ft. For car-shuttles, park second car at Wolf Creek North, TH37.

Map: Topaz Lake (for continuation backpacks south and west, reference Markleeville, Dardanelles Cone, and Sonora.)

H: Wolf Creek Meadow, 3 to 20 mi., 400 to 1800 ft.; Car-shuttle or loop hike via Murray Canyon and High Trail, 21 mi. 3700 ft., or via Carson River Trail, 24 mi., 3100 ft.

Wolf Creek runs north-south, with a number of trails into the Carson Iceberg Wilderness. You can pick your hike, from a family picnic walk to a full-on day trek or multi-day backpack. **At 2 mi. in**, the trail joins the creek at a scenic bluff. It then continues through cottonwood meadows, under siege from beavers, and climbs gradually through mixed conifers. **At 5 mi.**, just after a rocky gorge with junipers as its guardians, you'll come to the **Bull Canyon Trail**. **At 6 mi.** in, is a good lunch spot for day hikers, with views of Bull Peak and a cataract with falls.

Note: Heed private property in this area—a ranch inholding in the wilderness area.

GREG HAYES

Wolf Creek

Continuing south, in less than a mile you'll reach the lush upper reaches of Wolf Creek, where the **Elder Creek Trail** takes off and up to the west.

For the monster **loop hike or car-shuttle via Murray Canyon**, take the Murray trail east, beginning 7 mi. in, up and out of Wolf Creek into Falls Meadow. From there, proceed east to Soda Springs Ranger Station in Dumonts Meadow. From Dumonts, walk north 2.5 mi. to where the High Trail forks to the left, and the Carson River Trail forks right—both trails lead back to Wolf Creek North trailhead.

For non-loop hikers, stay on the Wolf Creek trail past the Murray Canyon trail junction. This trail leads to the **Pacific Crest Trail**. From the PCT, you can turn north toward Highland Lakes or Nobel Lake, or south toward **Golden Canyon** into Falls Meadow, or **PCT south** to Sonora Pass—although these options are more for backpackers.

BP: Your options are numerous: lots of space, trails, water, firewood, vistas, and connecting to higher elevations of the PCT. See hiking descriptions above. You can start at Wolf Creek South and, in a few nights, come out at the following trailheads: at Wolf Creek North, TH37, via Murray Canyon; or at Ebbetts Pass South, TH39, via Bull Canyon; or at Highland Lakes, TH40, via Elder Creek Trail; or at Little Antelope, TH48, via Murray Canyon and Poison Flat Trail from Soda Springs Ranger Station in Dumonts; or at Sonora Pass, TH51, via Golden Canyon to White Canyon South; or at Sonora Pass, via PCT south.

      If all this seems confusing, just pack into upper Wolf Creek and camp.

F: Fly-fishing in **Wolf Creek.** Walk the trail upriver from parking into Carson Iceberg Wilderness, for mostly rainbows. Or head downriver into Wolf Creek Meadow, for brook trout. You can also park at the north end of the meadow, at the bridge, and fish the rugged canyon downstream.

37.   WOLF CREEK NORTH   H, BP, MB, F

  Best For: Alpine meadows, early-season hiking with flowers, getting distance with limited climbing, horseback riding, backpack options.
  Park: Take Wolf Creek Road, 3 mi. south of jct. Hwys. 89/4. The road is unpaved after 2 mi. After dropping into Wolf Creek meadows, take the first left and continue 1.5 mi., not turning toward Dixon Mine, until reaching an improved trailhead parking area, which is set up for horse trailers. At 6300 ft.
  Map: Markleeville

H: Wolf Creek Lake, 1.5 mi., 600 ft.; Grays Crossing, 6 mi., 1300 ft.; Silver King Valley, 12 mi., 1400 ft.; High Trail to Dumonts Meadow loop, 15 mi., 2200 ft.

Wolf Creek Lake, which is over the saddle you climb from the trailhead, is an example of a lake transforming into a meadow. To **Grays Crossing**, continue 1.5 miles beyond the lake, then take a trail branching to left, downward, toward the East Carson River. Across the river—Grays Crossing—is Bagley Valley and a trail out to Hwy. 395 at TH45.

To **Silver King Valley**, take the right fork described above, not dropping to the river, and continuing for another 3 miles, along the river canyon. The trail reaches the green valley, with Silver King Creek snaking through it.

To take the **High Trail** to **Dumonts Meadow**, look for the trail just a couple hundred feet from the parking area, as it takes off up to the right, south. The High Trail climbs for several miles before dropping down at the north end of **Dumonts Meadow**. Here the High Trail joins the Carson River trail, south of Silver King. Turn left, or north, to walk the seven miles back via Silver King on the trail described above.

BP: A very user-friendly backpacking area, flat and sandy (decomposed granite) along the river. Good for young kids and short-trippers. Also an early-season choice for extended treks, many options are available. Some possible routes are south to Carson Falls, White Canyon and Sonora Pass; or to Hwy. 395 at Little Antelope via Poison Flat; or to Wolf Creek South via Murray Canyon.

Watch out: Creek crossings can be a problem during high-water years.

MB: In the spring, Wolf Creek Road is gated at Centerville campground due to snow, making this a route for mountain bikers who don't mind walking bikes over a few hundred feet of packed snow. You can ride into Wolf Creek Meadow and Dixon Mine.

F: The hike along **Upper East Carson** leads to some big pools holding cutthroat, rainbows and browns—beginning at Gray's Crossing and continuing to Silver King Valley, Dumonts Meadow and Falls Meadow. Great area for backpacking or horse-riding fishermen. Ditto for **Silver King Creek**.

Note: The river above Carson Falls is protected and closed to fishing.

38. EBBETTS PASS NORTH H, BP, MB, CC, B, F

Best for: Volcanic formations, easy trail through rough country, high-country wildflowers.

Park:	At Ebbetts Pass turnout on Hwy 4. At 8700 ft. *Note:* The PCT crosses Hwy. 4 about .25-mile east of the Ebbetts Pass turnout. The official PCT trailhead parking is about .5-mile east of Ebbetts, but this is not convenient for hikes north.
Map:	Markleeville

H: PCT north to Upper Kinney Lake, 2 mi., 300 ft.; Raymond Meadows, 7 mi., 500 ft.; Pennsylvania Creek, 13.5 mi., 1000 ft.; Raymond Lake, 21 mi., 1600 ft.

For **Upper Kinney Lake**, take a trail up and northerly from Ebbetts Pass, making sure you connect with PCT south by jogging a few hundred feet eastward from the turnout. **Raymond Meadows** features numerous brooks, willows and wildflowers beneath the volcanic buttresses of Reynolds Peak. You can't see Raymond Peak from here—a ridge intervenes. For **Pennsylvania Creek**, continue along the level and circuitous trail, around the craggy protuberances and into hidden forests.

The trail to **Raymond Lake**, doable as a day hike for the fittest of hikers, is more of the same: around volcanic ridges before coming clear around to the east side of Raymond. From here you climb an 800-foot ramp to the lake, a beautiful cirque beneath the many-toothed ridge of Raymond Peak.

Note: Raymond Lake is more readily accessed from TH19, Wet Meadows.

Watch-out: It's tempting to cut across one of the ridges that the trail goes around to get to Raymond Lake; but you may well encounter cliffs, loose rock and big drop-offs.

BP: In Raymond Meadows and Pennsylvania Creek, no problem finding out-of-the-way campsites with plenty of firewood and vistas galore. Raymond Lake, however, usually has packers at its 4 or 5 campsites.

MB: In spring, Ebbetts Pass road is gated, either down below at the Monitor Pass turnoff, or higher up at Silver Creek. Park at either gate and ride in along the river on pavement, avoiding the seasons rock-falls and perhaps pushing the bike over the occasional snow patch.

CC: After heavy winter snows, drive to the junction of Hwys. 4 and 89, where both roads are gated, and ski up toward Ebbetts Pass.

B: Kayakers and canoeists will find Kinney Reservoir a scenic, on-road spot to paddle.

F: **Kinney Reservoir**, which is on Hwy. 4 about 1 mile east of Ebbetts Pass, draws float tubers and casters looking for rainbows. Rainbows are also the most prevalent trout at **Kinney Lakes**, which can be reached via the above hiking description or by taking a trail beginning at Kinney Reservoir dam, 1 mile to **Lower Kinney Lake**.

39. EBBETTS PASS SOUTH H, BP, F

Best for: Big, wild Sierra feel, escarpments, vistas, wildflowers, mixed conifers.
Park: At Ebbetts Pass, Hwy. 4., in Pacific Crest Trail lot. At 8700 ft.
Note: Some Nobel Lake hikers park at Cadillac Curve, 1.5 west (up) from Silver Creek Campground; this option adds a mile or two on to the hike. For car-shuttle, park second car at Wolf Creek South, TH36.
Maps: Markleeville, plus Topaz Lake for car-shuttle.

H: Nobel Lake, 8 mi., 1800 ft.; Tryon Peak, 12 mi. (4 mi. off-trail), 2800 ft.; Bull Lake, 12 mi., 2000 ft.; Wolf Creek car-shuttle, 16 mi., 1500 ft.; Highland Peak, 14 mi. (5 mi. off-trail), 3900 ft.

The **Nobel Lake** hike has commanding vistas of the canyon and of giant Silver and Highland peaks. The walk in will please tree and flower fans. To reach **Tryon Peak,** with its fascinating geology and 360-degree view, take the trail southerly from Nobel Lake. From the saddle south of Nobel, leave the trail—which continues into Elder Creek and Paradise Valley—and make your way west and up, climbing steeply toward Tryon's southeast shoulder. You'll top out onto a sandy flat area with dwarf hemlocks and whitebark. Then proceed up the last few hundred feet of scree, heading due north now, to the moonscape top of Tryon Peak.

To scale **Highland Peak**, a murderous slog, take the Bull Canyon trail east from Nobel lake, around to the back side of the stand-alone ridge above the lake's east shore. Then begin the long ascent off-trail, over jagged footing, up Highland's southwest shoulder.

JOHN BARR

Crossing East Carson River

For the **Wolf Creek car-shuttle,** take the Bull Canyon trail from Nobel Lake, up and through the narrow, forested saddle. **Bull Lake** is a 2-mile side trip south off this trail, not far from the saddle. Once down to Wolf Creek, you'll meet the trail 5.5 miles from trailhead parking at TH36. This car-shuttle hike, one of Alpine's best, takes you through varied terrain and is not particularly difficult, in spite of the distances.

BP: Nobel Lake itself is not that great of a backpack lake. Check out the fanned-out drainage just south of the lake, or head to Bull Lake. Base camp here to loop hike on the Pacific Crest Trail toward Golden Canyon or Paradise Valley.

F: **Bull Lake,** about a 12-mile round-trip hike, is good fishing for cutthroat. A popular lake among backpackers with poles.

40. HIGHLAND LAKES H, BP, MB, B, F

Best for:	Variety of trees and flowers, numerous day hike and backpack destinations, mountain bike and horseback explorations.
Park:	Take Highland Lakes Road, off Hwy. 4, 2 mi. west of Ebbetts Pass. Go 5 mi., through Bloomfield Camp, to Highland Lakes. Park at east end of larger lake. At 8700 ft.
Maps:	Markleeville, Dardanelles Cone, Sonora

H: Upper Garner Meadow, 2 mi., 250 ft.; Asa Lake, 5 mi., 400 ft.; Paradise Valley, 13 mi., 1200 ft.; Carson Iceberg Meadow, 16.5 mi., 2200 ft.

In **Upper Garner Meadows,** just into the next drainage from the trailhead, are several lakelets at the headwaters of east-flowing Elder Creek. The trail to **Asa Lake** takes off to the northeast, about a mile from the trailhead, above the north end of Garner Meadows. On the way you'll cross the Pacific Crest Trail—which would give you vistas of Wolf Creek if you opted to take it south—and come to the junction for the Asa Lake trail. The lake is a .5-mile jog north. The Elder Creek trail continues through Wolf Creek Pass into the drainage, coming down east of the trail to Murray Canyon.

To reach **Paradise Valley,** continue south through Upper Garner Meadows. Don't take a trail forking right, or westerly, at the southern end of Garner Meadows. After several miles, take an east fork on the trail and follow north Disaster Creek into rugged Paradise Valley to the foot of Disaster Peak. This trail continues to join the PCT, high above Wolf Creek, and on the way to Golden Canyon.

To reach **Carson Iceberg Meadow,** continue south on the trail, losing elevation, following Disaster Creek. You may wish to stop up high, a mile or two from the meadow and view the Iceberg from on top.

Note: Iceberg Meadow can be reached more easily by driving to Clark Fork/Cottonwood Campground Road, 20 miles west of Sonora Pass off Highway 108. The trailhead is 9 miles in from Highway 108.

BP: With lots of middling ups and downs and a spider web of trails—and falling on four different topo maps—this area can be hard to navigate. Stay on trails. Consider a car-shuttle using Clark Fork road, described above, or a Wolf Creek trailhead, TH36 or TH37.

MB: Park at Hwy. 4, or at Bloomfield Camp 2 miles in. Excellent run into Highland Lakes, with side roads to explore.

B: Both Highland Lakes are good for serene, high-altitude kayaking and canoeing.

F: **Highland Lakes** are fished for brook trout. The road is usually open by mid-June. By stopping at Bloomfield Camp, 2 miles in from the highway, you can fish a fairly flat section of the **Mokelumne River** for rainbows and browns.

41. HERMIT VALLEY H, BP MB, F

Best for: Getaway river hikes with flowers and horseback rides.
Park: At Hermit Valley Campground, on Hwy. 4, 4 mi. west of Ebbetts Pass. At 7200 ft..
Map: Markleeville

H: Grouse Creek, 6 mi., 500 ft.; Deer Valley, 7 mi., 600 ft.; Stevenot Camp, 12 mi., 800 ft.

Grouse Creek trail takes off southeast from Hermit Valley on the south side of the highway. Follow the lush streamside to Willow Meadow, 3 miles in. Water-loving wildflowers will be pocketed along the margins of Grouse Creek throughout the summer.

For **Deer Valley** and **Stevenot Camp**, take the trail heading northwest on the north side of the highway. It begins by climbing and winding through varied terrain. The trail will turn northward, reaching the confluence of Blue and Deer creeks, which is in Deer Valley. From here to Stevenot you contour southwest, not following the drainage, until reaching the pleasant overlooks of the camp, with its surrounding lakelets and recognizable knob.

Local Lore: Members of the Murietta Gang are said to have whiled away hours resting up in the Deer Valley and Stevenot Camp area.

BP: The Mokelumne River provides a number of spots to get far away without going very far. But be careful: Snowshoe Thompson said Hermit Valley was the only place he ever got lost.

MB: Hermit Valley trailhead north to Deer Valley is the southern terminus of a crude road from Blue Lakes—a rugged bike ride. Another option is a hike 'n bike: Getting off the main trail quickly puts you into some of the Alpine's most remote country.

F: **North Fork of the Mokelumne River** passes under highway at Hermit Valley, a parking spot for two river fishing walks. One stretch to catch rainbow trout is downriver for about 1.5 miles from the road; lots of pools and white water—and rugged footing. A second spot is upriver from Hwy. 4, where the fishing is good for rainbows and brown trout, and the terrain easier to walk.

42. PACIFIC VALLEY H, BP, F

Best for:	Family picnic walk in search of flowers and peak views, horseback jaunts.
Park:	Take Pacific Valley Campground Road, south off Hwy. 4, 7 mi. west of Ebbetts Pass. Drive in 1.5 mi. At 7600 ft.
Maps:	Markleeville and Dardanelles Cone

H: Pacific Creek Meadow, 3.5 mi., 400 ft.

Pacific Creek Meadow is the water-sluiced clearing below Bull Run, Henry and Lookout peaks. Two streams meet, and both fall color and wildflowers are profuse in season. This is a destination that invites more energetic hikers to explore the environs while others catch up on some creek-side R&R.

BP: This trailhead offers options for southbound packers wishing to explore the low-elevation granitic moonscape of Dardanelles Cone. The Cone and environs is about 10 miles south of the trailhead, via Slaughter Canyon. Confused topography and manzanita can make this area a maze, but you will also find many tucked-away camp spots.

F: From the Pacific Valley Campground, walk **Pacific Creek**, casting for brook trout and some browns, along a 2-mile stretch. **Mosquito Lake**, a jewel right on Hwy. 4, 1.5 miles west of Pacific Valley, is a lake for brook trout.

43. LAKE ALPINE H, BP, MB, CC, B, F

Best for:	Picnic walks, walk-and-swim, paddling, out-of-the-way backpack lake, biking, taking in one of Bear Valley's events.
Park:	On Hwy. 4 at Lake Alpine, 16 mi. west of Ebbetts Pass, 7 mi. east of Bear Valley Resort. At 7300 ft. For Bull Run Lake, drive in 1 mile on

Stanislaus Meadow Road, south off Hwy. 4, 3.5 mi. east of Lake Alpine. At 7800 ft.

Maps: Dardanelles Cone and Markleeville

H: Duck Lake, 3 mi., 350 ft.; Bull Run Lake, 6.5 mi., 900 ft.

To **Duck Lake,** walk past cabins on Lake Alpine's east shore, continuing east and a little south. This hike is a favorite among lake dwellers. Hikers might also check out the trails from **Lake Alpine's southwest shore,** leading along a granite-banked stream—pools and troughs await dipping.

For **Bull Run Lake** follow the trail out of Stanislaus Meadow as it turns east up the beginnings of the Stanislaus River. Your path then climbs and twists to the south, through a different drainage, and finally ascending to the forested lake.

BP: Bull Run Lake is a full-service destination for backpackers, with some wild-country side trips for a layover day—Bull Run Peak, about a mile east is a challenging non-technical climb. South of Lake Alpine, backpackers will find granitic trails and camp spots with views of Dardanelles Cone.

MB: From Lake Alpine are a number of mountain bike paths, including one around the lake and one to Uttica Reservoir. Some of the riding is on Forest Service roads, some on bike paths. Bike rentals available in Bear Valley.

CC: Bear Valley Cross County and Adventure Center is located west of Lake Alpine (accessible only from the west during winter). The center has rentals and 65 kilometers of groomed track.

B: Sailing, kayaking and canoeing are popular on Lake Alpine. Granite formations protrude into the lake, making for many swimming and picnic spots.

F: **Lake Alpine** is big enough to get out in the middle and have plenty of space to fish, for rainbows and brookies.

44. LOOPE CANYON H, MB

Best for: Exploring on foot or by mountain bike, historic mining district, fall color picnics.

Park: Take Loope Canyon Road, 2 mi. east of jct. Hwys. 89/4. Drive in 1.5 mi. to Forest City Flat. At 6900 ft.

Map: Topaz Lake

H: Markleeville Lookout, 3 mi., 1000 feet; Haypress Flat, 6 mi., 1100 ft. (without doing lookout); Little Cottonwood Canyon, 12 mi., 2100 feet.

To reach **Markleeville Lookout**, take a left, west, option on the road, which will then cross the ephemeral Mogul Canyon drainage after .5-mile. Then look for a spur road to the left, or west again, that goes up to knob, which is the lookout.

To **Haypress Flat**, backtrack from the lookout, and continue north, ascending gradually and reaching a wide-open area with a spring and aspen. On the north end of Haypress are views of the Carson Valley.

Local Lore: Haypress Flat's aspen groves are known for artful Basque carvings from the late 1800s and early 1900s.

To **Little Cottonwood Canyon,** take a trail to the southwest out of Haypress, descending for 1.5 miles–and avoiding a north-heading trail 1 mile from Haypress. The Little Cottonwood trail takes off north, descending, and ending after 1.5 miles. Instead of going to Cottonwood Canyon, you could continue west and connect with the Barney Riley Jeep Trail and come out at Hangmans Bridge, TH32.

Watch out: Exploring old mines can be dangerous; use caution and heed signs.

MB: Park at Hwy. 89 at Loope Canyon Road. System of old roads runs through historic Mogul Mining District, including to Haypress Flat, as described above. By veering right at Forest City Flat, you'll go by Morningstar Mine, and by taking a right-turn option, to the east, you can connect with roads that lead to Leviathan Mine and continue down 7 miles to Hwy. 395 south of Gardnerville, Nevada.

Or take a southerly fork that comes out on Hwy. 89, above Heenan Lake. From the highway, coast down to the Loope Canyon Road. You can also reach the Barney Riley Jeep Trail via Haypress Flat, as described in hiking section above. This is a big enough area to get lost in, but not so big that you can't pedal yourself out of it.

45. HEENAN LAKE H, BP, MB, B, F

Best for:	Where Jeffrey pine belt gives way to Great Basin, early wildflowers, long walks with little elevation, on foot, bike or horseback.
Park:	At Heenan Lake, on Hwy. 89, 4 mi. east of jct. 4/89. At 7100 feet.
Map:	Topaz Lake

H: Bagley Valley, 5 mi., 300 ft.; Grays Crossing, 9 mi., 900 ft; Silver King Valley, 12 mi., 800 ft.

To **Bagley Valley**, an open sweep of sagebrush—but with enough water for wildflowers early in the season—take the trail along the west shore of Heenan Lake, heading south. To **Grays Crossing**, which connects with Wolf Creek North, TH37, continue south through Bagley Valley. You'll descend gradually before turning west through an obvious opening in the land form, at a road fork. Grays Crossing is through the East Carson River. If the river is too deep to cross here, don't plan on crossing it.

To **Silver King Valley**, bear left, south, at the road fork at the southern end of Bagley Valley. The additional 2-mile walk takes you into an emerald meadow, where the Silver King Creek makes lazy bends and meets the East Carson.

Local Lore: Vaquero Camp, bunkhouse for cowboys of yesteryear, is part of a ranching history that predates the mining districts of the 1860s. It makes a scenic rest stop.

BP: Bagley is a good ending trailhead for car-shuttle day hikes or shorter pack trips that begin at Wolf Creek North, TH37, Wolf Creek South, TH36, or Little Antelope, TH48. With low elevations, this area is open early. A great variety of flora and fauna to be found in this region.

MB: Open terrain, although clay soil and coconut rocks can make for tough going in places. Heenan can be a part of an adventurous loop ride that begins at Monitor Pass, TH46, though you may end up carrying your bike overhead through brush in some spots.

B: Heenan is a good-sized pond to paddle, with Great Basin mountain scenery.

F: **Heenan Lake** is the only Lahontan cutthroat stock lake in California. To protect this rare breed, special restrictions apply: Open from the Friday before Labor Day until the end of October, fishing only Friday through Sunday from sunrise to sunset. Catch-and-release fishing with no live bait, single, barbless hook.

46. MONITOR PASS H, MB, CC, F

Best for: Fall color, quick hike to big peak, Sierran crest views, high rides for horses and bikes.

Park: For Leviathan Peak, drive in .5-mi. on peak road, 1 mi. east of Monitor Pass on Hwy. 89. For other hikes, park where unpaved road 083 meets Hwy. 89, .75 mi. west of Monitor Pass. For car-shuttle, park second car at Indian Springs Road 085, 2 mi. east of Monitor Pass. At 8300 ft.

Map: Markleeville

H: Leviathan Peak, 2 mi., 1200 ft; Leviathan circumnavigation car-shuttle, 5 miles (7 mi. without car shuttle), 300 feet; Company Meadow, 4 mi., 400 ft.

Monitor Pass Road

The walk up to **Leviathan Peak** is on a trail along open sage slopes, often replete with dwarf wildflowers and Alpine's signature flower, mule ears. The lookout station at the top provides a view in all directions, taking a wide-angle on the Sierran Crest, bucolic Antelope Valley and Topaz Lake.

The **clockwise trip around Leviathan,** beginning northward from the parking, is a fairly flat walk, the only climb over a low saddle of High Peak to the northwest of Leviathan. As you continue around, look for Big Spring, a sleeper lunch spot. Then follow the road to circle around the mountain to the highway. You can walk back along the road if a car-shuttle isn't convenient, adding 2 miles to the hike.

Company Meadows is south of Highway 395 from the trailhead at road 083. A series of roads and trails squirm through piñon and aspens, as well as other pine and fir. One destination is a knob due south, from which you can view Slinkard Valley below treacherous cliffs to the east. In this direction is Dump Canyon, which camels were cajoled into descending in the old days. (See Introduction to Markleeville region.) Bagley Valley is to the west, down steeply but walkable—not counting brush.

MB: Monitor Pass has numerous mountain biking roads to explore, including those mentioned in hiking description. Indian Springs Road continues for a number of miles north, and can actually be ridden down to Hwy. 395. From Company Meadows, you can ride down toward Heenan Lake, although doing so requires bushwhacking for several hundred feet. In the spring, when the road is gated at the junction of Highways 4 and 89, you can ride in on the pavement up to Monitor.

CC: Hwy. 89 is closed for winter at the junction of Hwy. 4. When the road is first opened in the late spring, skiing on top is excellent, if the winter's snowpack cooperates. Also, before the road is opened, during heavy winters or after a storm, park at the gate and ski up the highway.

F: **Mountaineer Creek** will be a pleasant surprise for fly-fishermen. Take Indian Springs Road 085 and park at Big Spring, just after a left-fork. Fish the creek down and north from the spring.

47. SLINKARD VALLEY   H, BP, MB, F

Best for: Getting a feel for the purple sage, exploring cowboy artifacts, riding horses and bikes.

Park: Take dirt road, off Hwy. 89, 3.5 mi. east of jct. with Hwy. 395. Park at gate, less than .5-mi. from the highway. At 6000 ft.

Map: Topaz Lake

H: From 5 to 15 mi., 200 to 1000 ft.

Slinkard Valley is the sublime hanging valley best viewed from Hwy. 89 east of Monitor Pass as you drop down the east side of the Sierra. Hiking on Slinkard's gated road due south allows you to choose the length of your hike. You can also explore a number of side trails and roads into the valley's several ravines.

Local Lore: The remains of an ingenious catchment and irrigation system, as well as a number of outbuildings and mine structures, are to be found along the breadth and depth of Slinkard Valley.

BP: Slinkard can be used to access Upper Fish Valley and Llewellyn Falls, via Rodriquez Flat. But a more direct access to those areas is from Little Antelope, TH48. Slinkard is more commonly a trip ending trailhead for backpackers.

MP: Though the surface is rocky and rutted in places, mountain biking may be the best way to see all that's worth seeing in a day. A great place to get away and mountain bike-hike.

F: Fly fishermen are apt to find a treasure of hungry brookies hanging out among the watercress in the small pools of **Slinkard Valley Creek.**

Sonora

Like Markleeville, Bridgeport is a California town that by quirk of geographical survey wound up on the east side of the Sierra. Most people debated, in 1875, where California ended and Nevada began. Then rich ore was discovered and better surveys decided the issue. Even so, Bridgeport faced stiff competition for the honor of county seat from several tent-cities pitched on top of mining claims.

Emigrant Wilderness

Unlike Markleeville, this region has never seen much traffic, aside from local miners in the late 1800s. Sonora Pass is closed in the winter and the nearest trans-Sierra route is 80 miles north, after making it through rugged Walker River Canyon. The Great Basin is to the east and the Sierra juts to the west.

But the same geographic conditions that have historically created economic isolation now provide the region with a wealth of recreational tourism. As you take Highway 395 down the east Sierra, every 15 or 25 miles, a road leads into a hanging valley of the Sierra Nevada. Sonora Pass, Walker River, Little Walker River, Twin Lakes, Buckeye Creek, and Green Lakes are all entrances to mountainous watersheds and river valleys. All drain into the Great Basin via northern flowing Walker River, which is the world's longest landlocked riparian environment.

Thousands of years ago, ancient peoples roamed the Sonora region, then a central part of the Lahontan Lakeland Empire—a plentiful region of woodlands and huge, interconnected lakes that stretched from Pyramid Lake north of Reno to the Colorado River. Although these lakelands have dried out to form high desert, many primary lakes remain, shrunken, but still large. Walker, Topaz and Bridgeport lakes are three. These catchments for Sierran snowmelt provide a safe haven for millions of migrating waterfowl, as well as open water for boaters.

The ancestry of these ancient people can be traced through the language they spoke—Hokan—to the Paiute Indians who were in the region when the first European people came through in 1833, as part of an expedition led by Captain Joseph Walker. No Mother Lode or Comstock was discovered in this region to create a massive boom, although Bodie, ten miles south of Bridgeport, was a thriving mining town for a decade beginning in 1877. Bodie has been preserved almost intact as a State Park. (See Driving Tour 4.)

Part of Mono County's high country was annexed into Alpine County by the California Legislature in 1864. People have long memories. Twenty years later, when Alpine was down in the dumps due to the Silver bust, Mono hatched a political scheme to get its portion back, and then some.

When a murderer was on trial in Markleeville, his Mono county attorney applied successfully for a change of venue, arguing no fair trial could be had in Markleeville, which was true due to a number of eye witnesses to the mishap. Transporting the prisoner and paying for a lengthy trial would've bankrupted Alpine County at the time, thus facilitating Mono's takeover. Fearing this, a group of Alpiners cut through the red tape. They caught up with the Mono-bound prisoner a mile south of Markleeville and did frugal justice at soon-to-be-named Hangmans Bridge.

This Mono-Alpine sibling rivalry was ameliorated in 1954 when Monitor Pass was completed, ending the isolation between the two, and making it at last possible to drive to and fro without going into Nevada.

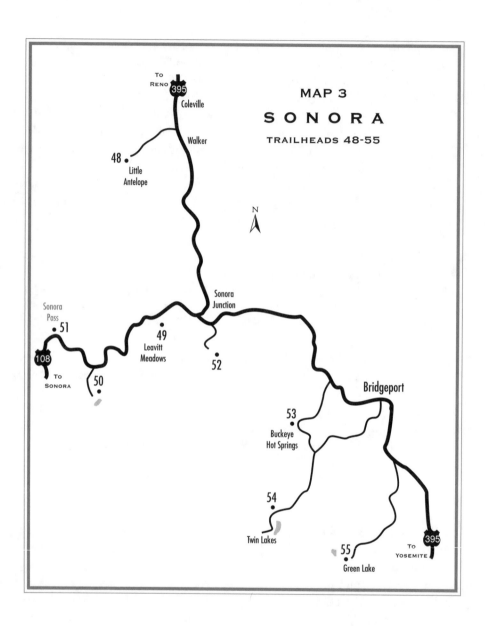

MAP 3

SONORA

TRAILHEADS 48-55

To Reno 395

Coleville

Walker

48 Little Antelope

N

Sonora Junction

Sonora Pass 51

49 Leavitt Meadows

108

52

To Sonora

50

Bridgeport

53 Buckeye Hot Springs

54

Twin Lakes

55 Green Lake

To Yosemite 395

TRAILHEAD DESCRIPTIONS

48. LITTLE ANTELOPE PACK STATION   H, BP, MB, F

Best for: East Alpine high country, early season backpacking and summer horse trips to river meadows, wildflower ridges.

Park: Take unpaved road to Little Antelope Pack Station/Mill Canyon Road, off Hwy. 395 a few miles north of Walker. Drive in (and up) 7 miles. At 8200 feet.

Maps: Topaz Lake and Sonora Pass

H: Slinkard Valley overlook, 3 mi., 600 ft.; Llewellyn Falls loop, 14.5 mi., 2200 ft.

The **Slinkard Valley overlook** is a walk up from the pack station through forest. After the initial climb, you come to an exposed area, which features a display of sun-loving wildflowers, as the trail contours west and south.

For the **Llewellyn loop,** which will take you hill-and-dale through a number of ecosystems, take a south-heading trail from the exposed area, toward **Corral Valley trail.** You drop into smallish Corral Valley and out its narrow saddle, continuing south into **Coyote Valley,** which features a number of junipers. In Coyote Valley, take a left (southeast) trail at a junction, taking you down into **Upper Fish Valley** at Connels Cow Camp, .5-mile above **Llewellyn Falls.**

Go downstream—which is Silver King Creek, the home of the protected Paiute Trout—past Llewellyn Falls and into **Lower Fish Valley** and continue into **Long Valley,** another meadow cleaved by the creek.

About .75-mile from the southern end of Long Valley, at a creek crossing that is the junction of a trail to Poison Flat, take the **"Driveway Trail"** heading up and to the northeast. The Driveway Trail takes you back to the junction of the Corral Valley trail.

BP: Fish Valleys and upper Silver King are comfortable, scenic packing areas, open early in the season and popular with horse campers later in the year. Llewellyn Falls is a good base camp to explore upper Silver King Creek or dramatic Whitecliff Lake. This trailhead also is a starting point for 1-to 3-night car-shuttle trips that start out heading easterly via Snodgrass Creek or Poison Flat to Dumonts Meadow, and then go northerly, coming out at either Heenan Lake, TH45, or the Wolf Creek, TH36 or TH37.

MB: Park a second car at Slinkard Valley, TH47. From 1 mile east of Rodriquez Flat/ Little Antelope Pack Station, take an old road, starting out on a steep decline, and then heading north 13 miles north through Slinkard Valley. Make sure you start out on the right road: There are spur roads to mines, which are east of the road you want, although these road are options to ride instead of going into Slinkard. Travel in pairs on this trip and be prepared to walk the bike in places.

F: Horsemen and backpackers with poles like **Silver King Creek in Lower Fish Valley** and **Long Valley**. Downstream, a few miles north of Long Valley from the Snodgrass Creek Trail—walking down from Rodriguez Flat—is **Silver King Valley**, another good fishing section. This is near where Silver King Creek meets the East Carson above Grays Crossing. **Poison Lake**—2 miles west and up from Long Valley—is known for good camping and catching the limit.

Note: Other areas closed to fishermen to protect Paiute Trout habitat are Corral Valley, Coyote Valley and Silver King Creek above Llewellyn Falls, including Upper Fish Valley.

49. LEAVITT MEADOWS H, BP, F

Best for: Mid-elevation backpacking, long hikes with minimal elevation, river meadows, wildflowers, river dipping, horseback trips.
Park: At Leavitt Meadows Pack Station/trailhead parking, on Hwy. 108, 6 mi. west of Hwy. 395. At 7100 ft..
Maps: Sonora and Tower Peak

H: Roosevelt and Lane lakes, 5 mi., 400 ft.; Poore Lake loop, 6 mi., 300 ft.; Fremont Lake, 12 mi., 1100 ft.; Upper Paiute Meadows, 20 mi., 1200 ft.

The trail from Leavitt Meadows follows the Walker River upstream to its headwaters. After crossing through sage lands bordering Leavitt Meadow, the trail ascends gradually.

To **Poore Lake loop**, take a left-forking trail, .25-mile after the trail begins its switchbacks, and make your way through statue-like rock formations. Secret Lake, a small one, lies about .25-mile west of Poore's southern tip. To return, take an old road down the east shore of Poore Lake. You'll travel through sagebrush above the Leavitt Meadow trail—make sure to take a left-forking option as you near the highway.

To reach forested and popular **Roosevelt** and **Lane lakes**, which are separated by a long stone's throw, take the right-forking trail, the main trail, as you ascend from Leavitt Meadows. You won't see the lakes until you come upon them. To **Fremont Lake**, take a climbing, west-bearing trail, 2-plus miles south of these lakes. For **Paiute Meadow**, the lush valley with dramatic views southward of the craggy peaks of northern Yosemite, continue along the river trail, south.

BP: Roosevelt and Lane lakes are destinations for families with younger children. Fremont Lake makes for a first-night lake for packers headed west toward Emigrant Wilderness or Helen and Mary lakes of northern Yosemite. Upper Paiute Meadows is excellent for fishermen and as a base camp for hikes to Kirkwood Creek and Tower Lake. Via Paiute Meadows, you can also come out, on 4- to 5-night trips, at Buckeye Hot Springs, TH53, or Twin Lakes, TH54.

F: The **Walker River** will yield trout for fly-fishermen, beginning in Leavitt Meadow just south of the trailhead. **Roosevelt** and **Lane lakes** also have fish, but see a number of fishermen. Backpackers who like to fish should bring a pole to **Upper Paiute Meadows**, where the Walker River makes big sweeps.

50. LEAVITT LAKE H, BP, MB, B, F

Best for:	A peak hike that makes you feel like you're flying, quick entry into high back country.
Park:	Turn on Leavitt Lake Road off Hwy. 108, 10 mi. west of junction with Hwy. 395. Drive in 3.5 mi. to Leavitt Lake—on a road often not advisable for 2-wheel drive; inquire locally. At 9500 ft.
Maps:	Sonora and Tower Peak

H: Leavitt Lake Pass, 2 mi., 1000 ft.; Big Sam, 11 mi., 3200 ft.

The short trail to **Leavitt Lake Pass** is a butt-kicker right out of the car, climbing up and south from the parking area on the east shore of Leavitt Lake. You are rewarded with a commanding view of Sierran peaks to the south, as if gigantic storm-tossed waves were frozen in time.

To **Big Sam**, drop down the pass to the upper reaches of Kennedy Meadow Creek. From the pass you drop down considerably before contouring around and heading up the shoulder of Big Sam. Follow the trail—an old mining road that is a monument to cowboy engineering—up to Big Sam. From the near 11,000-foot, bare-topped peak, you get the most diverse vistas possible: the granite sheets of the Emigrant Wilderness, severe red slopes of the Hoover, alpine meadows, and granite crags of northern Yosemite.

Watch out: Mineralized Big Sam draws lightning; late afternoon is peak time for summer storms.

BP: Leavitt Lake trailhead gets you deep into the back country in a short time. Destinations include Emigrant Wilderness high country and Helen Lake area of northern Yosemite. The upper reaches of Kennedy Creek—sometimes called Hollywood Basin—which is down the backside of Leavitt Lake Pass, provides a sheltered, first-night camp spot, with reliable water.

MB: Park at the highway and ride into Leavitt Lake. Also, the trail out of Leavitt Lake is national forest, between Emigrant and Hoover Wilderness, making it possible to get to Leavitt Pass.

B: Leavitt Lake is like a water-filled crater on some other planet, with mineralized peaks ringing it. Kayakers will enjoy taking a float.

F: Pulling a trailer into **Leavitt Lake** is a risky proposition, but many fishermen have good luck from craft on this lake.

RICHARD HARVEY

Trout Dinner

51. SONORA PASS H, BP

Best for: Notable peak, variety of wildflowers, linking up with long, north-
south pack trips.
Park: At Sonora Pass, Hwy. 108, 14 mi. west of jct. Hwy. 395. At 9600 ft.
Map: Sonora Pass.

H: Sonora Peak, 6.5 mi. (1.5 mi. off-trail), 1800 feet; Wolf Creek Lake, 7 mi.,
1200 ft.

For **both hikes**, start out north on the PCT, ascending immediately as you switchback
westerly and then easterly and finally north, through lichen-splotched rock formations of
the massive mountain. To climb **Sonora Peak**, head off-trail about .5-mile after the trail
turns north—you may find a sketchy trail—walking due west. Sonora Peak has a comfortable rock shelter on top and 360-degree views, since no other peak is nearby.

For **Wolf Creek Lake**, stay on the PCT north, as you walk up and over the east shoulder
of Sonora Peak. You'll see the lake below as the trail drops down to it—either take the trail
or traverse down off-trail. Wolf Creek Lake—different from the lake of the same name
near Markleeville—is a good first-night camp for late-starting trips.

Note: At 11,462 feet, Sonora Peak is the highest peak in Alpine County—the Alpine and
Mono county boundary line runs through the top of the peak, as does the boundary
between Toiyabe and Stanislaus national forests.

BP: Sonora Pass gives you a high-elevation start for 3- to 5-night car-shuttle trips
headed to either Wolf Creek via White Canyon/East Carson Trail, TH36; Ebbetts
Pass via the PCT, TH39; or Little Antelope via White Canyon and Poison Flat,
TH48.

52. LITTLE WALKER RIVER H, BP, MB, F

Best for: High-meadow canyon, hidden hikes, horseback and mountain biking.
Park: Turn south on Obsidian Campground Road, 1 mi. south on Hwy.
395 from jct. Hwys. 395/108. Keep right, drive 3 mi. to Obsidian
Campground. For Emma Lake, turn right across bridge, go 2.5 mi. up
to Stockade Flat. At 8500 ft. For Burt Canyon and Anna Lake, stay
left, not crossing bridge, and drive 1.5 mi. to Hoover Wilderness
trailhead parking. At 8100 ft.
Maps: Fales Hot Springs, Matterhorn, Tower Peak (This is one of those pesky
areas that falls in the corner of topo maps.)

H: Emma Lake, 2.5 mi., 1000 ft.; Mount Emma, 4 mi. (3 mi. off-trail), 2400 ft.; Burt Canyon, 10 mi., 1200 ft.; Anna Lake, 15 mi., 2800 ft.; Paiute Pass, 13 mi., 2900 ft.

Emma Lake is a short but steep walk through the forest. From the trailhead, you climb fairly steeply, on a road for a while, through mixed conifers not catching a glimpse of the lake until you are upon it. By scrambling up the steep ridge to Emma's southwest you can get some views of the West Walker drainage.

Mount Emma, at 10,525 feet, is .5-mile southwest of the lake. To climb Mount Emma, go up the steep draw due south of Emma Lake, reaching a saddle. From the saddle, walk up the peak along its southwest shoulder. A stand-alone peak, Emma gives you a circular view taking in both the silvery Great Basin and the deep greens of Upper Paiute Meadows.

To **Burt Canyon**, starting at a different parking area, you walk past private cabin in-holdings and some huge junipers, and into the Hoover Wilderness. Great Basin flora gives way to aspen and conifers as you climb moderately but steadily, passing a large beaver pond, crossing the drainage—the Little Walker can be a problem to get across early in the year—and veering westerly. Burt Canyon is high meadow, fringed by varieties of fir and pine, with 11,500-foot Flatiron Butte and Hanna Mountain looking down from its south-ernmost reaches.

To reach **Anna Lake**, take a trail to the west, where a creek drops into Burt Canyon about 1.5 miles from the northern end of the canyon. It's a steady hump up to Anna, which will often be frozen well into June.

To **Paiute Pass**, look for a drainage to the west at the northern end of Burt Canyon—just as you get into an open area with views. Proceeding up the steep drainage, you climb a sketchy trail to 10,300-foot Paiute Pass. From a windswept ridge are spectacular views west.

BP: Burt Canyon is an ideal destination, for an in-and-out, or two-night trip.

MB: Park at Hwy. 395. The roads mentioned in the parking directions are all good for bikers. In addition, check out Molybdenite Creek, which is a left-forking option at Obsidian Campground. Wheeler Flat Road, which is a left fork just .5-mile from the highway, connects with roads that head easterly coming out after six or seven miles at Highway 395 at the Buckeye Hot Springs Road. Also, explore a whole other network of BLM roads on the other side of Hwy. 395—toward Burcham Flat.

Watch out: This is big country, remember where the car is.

F: For fly-fishermen willing to walk, **Little Walker River** in **Burt Canyon** is a sleeper for big brookies. Also try the beaver ponds, a couple miles from the trailhead. Catch-and-release recommended.

53. BUCKEYE HOT SPRINGS H, BP, MB, F

Best for:	Fall color, soak and hike or pedal into wild country.
Park:	Two ways into Buckeye Campground: One is off Twin Lakes Road, out of Bridgeport; drive in 7 mi. paved, turn right toward Buckeye and drive 3 mi. unpaved. The second way in is off Hwy. 395, 4 mi. north of Bridgeport; turn on Buckeye Road, across from an old ranger station, and drive in unpaved road through piñon forest, 3.5 mi. to campground. At 7300 ft. The unimproved hot springs is down from the road, on the river, .5-mi. east of the campground.
Map:	Matterhorn Peak

H: Buckeye Creek to Big Meadow, 10 mi., 500 ft.; The Roughs, 18 mi., 1100 ft.; Eagle Creek, 7 mi., 1900 ft.

For **Big Meadow**, follow Buckeye Creek through a sage-belt valley, with pockets of cottonwoods and aspen, climbing slightly, bearing southwest. More conifers join the landscape and a creek drops in from the north at Big Meadow. To reach the beginning of **The Roughs**, walk 3 more miles, ascending gradually and entering the aptly named craggy passageway to the Hoover Wilderness.

For **Eagle Creek**, a rugged, no-exit drainage for Eagle, Victoria (11,732 feet) and Robinson peaks, take the trail southwest from the campground that starts climbing right off the bat, following Eagle Creek. Lots of water in this wild country.

BP: This seldom-used trailhead is an entry or exit point for 3- or 4-night car-shuttle trips either southward to Twin Lakes, TH54, via Peeler, or northward to Leavitt Meadows, TH49, or Leavitt Lake, TH50, via Upper Paiute Meadows.

MB: Park at the unpaved sections of either of the two ways into Buckeye described in parking section above, and pedal past the campground up Buckeye Creek. Or, you might want to drive into the campground, ride up Buckeye Creek, stash the bikes and hike into The Roughs.

F: **Buckeye Creek** is an under-used fly-fishermen's waterway.

54. TWIN LAKES H, BP, B, F

Best for: Midsummer, High Sierra lake hikes, backpackers' entry point.
Park: At Mono Village Resort, 12 mi. from Bridgeport on Twin Lakes Road, off Hwy. 395. At 7200 ft.
Map: Matterhorn Peak

H: Barney Lake, 7.5 mi., 1100 ft; Peeler Lake, 15.5 mi., 2200 ft.; Crown Lake, 15 mi., 2300 ft.; Horse Creek, 7 mi., 1800 ft.

To **Barney Lake,** tromp through the campground and enter the Hoover Wilderness, beginning a gradual climb, at first through sage country and then into aspen and conifers. Steep cliffs on either side plunge into Barney's deep blue waters.

To **Peeler Lake**, take the trail along the west shore of Barney Lake, passing the scenic rocky bench that sits above the lake's south shore. Continue along Robinson Creek through an intervening valley, crossing the creek. Here you begin some serious climbing, crossing the creek again, before reaching a trail junction—where you go right to Peeler Lake or left to Crown. The trail to Peeler Lake continues upward through forested granite outcroppings until reaching cobalt-blue Peeler, perched smack on the edge of Yosemite. Peeler is one of the only lakes whose waters drain both sides of the crest.

To **Crown Lake**, also up a fair distance from the junction, make your way past some small lakes—warm for swimming—and then up the last ramp to the lake.

The **Horse Creek** trail heads due south from the west end of Twin Lakes. You climb steeply through rugged country toward the north side of Sawtooth Ridge—the signature ridge visible from Highway 395 at Bridgeport. Horse Creek is the confluence of three short streams which are fed by a half-dozen mini-glaciers held by Sawtooth Ridge.

Note: Matterhorn Peak is just southwest from the top of the Horse Creek trail, but don't plan on climbing it—or getting through the ridge from this side—unless you have wings or technical gear.

BP: Twin Lakes trailhead gets you deep into the Sierra, to bona fide beautiful country with many options. On 4- to 6-day car-shuttle treks, you can curl north from Peeler to Buckeye, TH53, or Leavitt Meadows, TH49. From Crown Lake, head south toward Virginia Lakes, TH56, or Lower Tuolumne, TH61. The bench above the south shore of Barney Lake is a scenic first-night camp. The trail from Crown Lake takes you down the backside of Sawtooth Ridge and through Burro Pass to Matterhorn Canyon.

B: Twin Lakes are large with deep blue waters and peaks rising steeply. You may wish to put in at the east end of Twin Lakes—at Lower Twin Lakes Campground—and paddle the three miles to the west shore of Upper Twin Lake. To do so, you'll have to portage the short distance between the two lakes.

F: **Twin Lakes** has boat launch facilities for deeper-water fishermen. The popularity of the campground is due in large part to lake fishing. **Barney Lake** is a destination for fly-casters.

Matterhorn Canyon

55. GREEN CREEK H, BP, MB, F

Best for: Fall color, car campers, day hikes into Hoover Wilderness, room to roam on horses and bikes.

Park: Take unpaved flat Green Lakes Road, 4 mi. south of Bridgeport on Hwy. 395. Park 8 mi. in at Green Creek Campground (avoiding fork to Virginia Lakes). At 8300 ft.

Map: Tuolumne Meadows

H: Green Lake, 4.5 mi., 700 ft.; West Lake, 7.5 mi., 1700 ft.; East Lake, 8 mi., 1200 ft.; Gilman Lake, 12 mi., 1400 ft.

Green Lake is a short walk that gives you a good feel for the Hoover Wilderness—pointed, mineral peaks with grand, steep shoulders dropping into lakes. A trail to Virginia Pass runs along the lake's east shore heading steeply up Glines Canyon.

To **West Lake**, take the right, westerly, fork of the trail at Green Lake's northwest shore. Three small lakes—Berona Lake and Par Value Lakes, lie just west of West Lake. Climb off-trail up the stream feeding the lake's west shore to reach Berona Lake. Par Value Lakes are a short distance, but around an escarpment, south of Berona Lake. This is a short but demanding side-trip.

Hikers to **East Lake** and **Gilman** need to take the southerly fork at Green Lake. Just as you get to East Lake, a trail forks to the right. This trail, an option to continuing to Gilman Lake, climbs steeply to a high saddle between Gabbro and Page peaks, and to a hidden lakelet held in a small basin. Gilman is an easy walk from East Lake—continuing south on the trail, you'll pass tiny Nutter Lake along the way.

BP: A 2-night, car-shuttle trip, with a second car at Virginia Lakes, TH56, is a natural. The Hoover, which flanks the east side of northern Yosemite, is not hugely popular among packers, but the topography described above makes for precious few places to pitch a tent.

MB: Park near the highway and ride Green Lakes Road, with an option of exploring the road to Virginia Lakes and other unsigned roads. You can also ride (up!) to the junction of Virginia Lakes Road, out to Hwy. 395, and down Conway Summit on 395—including about 10 miles downhill on the main highway.

F: Along **Green Creek** are a number of spots to car camp and walk the creek, fly-casting mainly for rainbow and cutthroat trout. **West Lake** is probably the best to shore-cast, although fishermen try their luck at all the lakes mentioned in the hiking section above.

Stamp Mill near Green Creek

Yosemite

Lower Tuolumne River

After geologic upheavals and glacial carvings, and centuries of habitation by American Indians, Yosemite Valley was discovered by Europeans in 1851. The majesty of the valley inspired the National Parks system, as well as a whole school of American painters and photographers. Now each year millions of admirers are drawn to the high country of Yosemite, Tuolumne Meadows, which over-looks Half Dome and other fabled monoliths of the valley.

Yosemite Valley is the largest gathering of people east of Stockton and Sacramento, for hundreds of miles, and surely the most cosmopolitan, with visitors from throughout the world. Day-trippers from Markleeville can drive to valley viewpoints in about two hours, making it possible to enjoy the park without having to endure what can be over-crowding in the valley below.

Water from the Yosemite high country forms into the Merced River in Yosemite Valley—via numerous falls that are among the world's highest. The Tuolumne River flows into Hetch Hetchy Valley which is parallel to the north of Yosemite Valley.

In Tuolumne Meadows, with a base elevation of about 9,000 feet, peaks were taller than the glaciers, so that their shoulders and saddles were scoured smooth as the ice moved by over the centuries, but their tops remained fancifully twisted and pointed. Polished granite bedrock of the high country also makes for streams with clear pools and unusual sprays of roostertailing white water.

Thanks to John Muir, Joseph LeConte, Clarence King and other naturalists and hikers, Yosemite became the first National Park. It is a testament not only to America's love of its natural treasures, but also, today, of how these treasures are worth more in economic terms when preserved. Muir and others failed in an attempt to prevent a dam in Hetch Hetchy Valley, said to be as magnificent.

To the west of Yosemite, at Mono Lake, naturalists similarly failed initially in at-tempts to prevent water exportation from harming the east Sierran ecosystem. But in recent years, the Mono Lake Committee was able to persuade federal courts that the lake's waters must be substantially restored, a decision that must have sent smiles from on high from Muir. The decision also has given millions of tourists a place to behold and explore. Migrating birds presumably are also much happier.

Hikes north and south out of Tuolumne Meadows give you high-country access without having to make that first 3,000-foot hump up that is typical of east Sierra trailheads as you go further south. Tioga Pass is the most southerly through route in the Sierra.

Yosemite is bordered by three Wilderness Areas: Emigrant, Hoover and Ansel Adams. Several trails run north-south through the Yosemite high-country, all interconnected, making it a hiker's park with unlimited options.

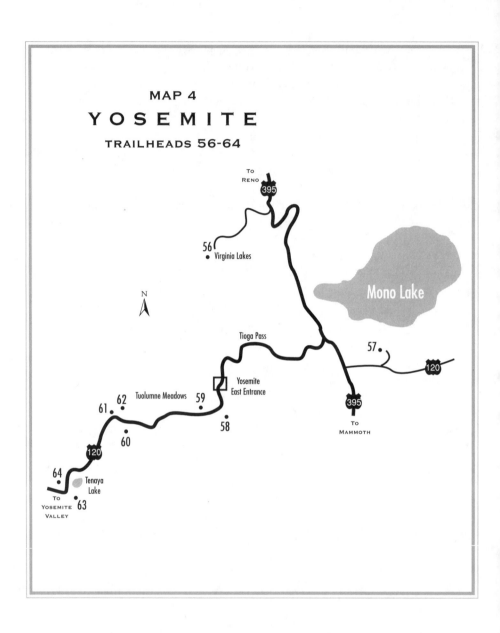

MAP 4

YOSEMITE

TRAILHEADS 56-64

To
Reno
395

56
Virginia Lakes

Mono Lake

N

Tioga Pass

57

120

Yosemite
East Entrance

Tuolumne Meadows 59

62
61
58
395

60

To
Mammoth

120

64
Tenaya
Lake
To
Yosemite 63
Valley

56. VIRGINIA LAKES H, BP, B, F

Best for:	Getting deep into high country on a day hike, vistas of Hoover Wilderness and extreme north Yosemite, paddling and pedaling.
Park:	Take Virginia Lakes Road off Hwy. 395 at Conway Summit, about halfway between Bridgeport and Lee Vining. Drive in 6 mi. to trailhead parking at Virginia Lakes. At 9800 ft.
Map:	Tuolumne Meadows

H: Frog Lakes, 4 mi., 900 ft.; Summit Lake Saddle, 6.5 mi., 1100 ft.; Summit Lake, 12 mi., 2200 ft.; Hoover Lakes, 12 mi., 2200 ft.

Frog Lakes, along with **Cooney** and **Blue lakes**, are a series of pools set in dwarf vegetation beneath mega Virginia Crest. You will pass these lakes, beginning with Blue Lake just as you climb gradually from the trailhead. Be careful not to stray onto fishermen's trails near Frog Lakes—the **Summit Lake Saddle** trail veers out the southwest quadrant of the lake basin.

To reach the saddle and **Summit Lake**, you take switchbacks on the face of the breathtaking (in more ways than one) pass, and then more switchbacks down the west side. Below the west side of the pass is a basin perennially gushing snowmelt from various fissures. At a trail juncture in this basin, take the west-leading trail, up some more, to Summit Lake. You'll want to walk to the lake's western shore to view the upper reaches of Spiller Creek and Return Canyon of northern Yosemite.

To reach **Hoover Lakes,** take the northerly trail when you reach the basin, heading down a mile or more, between very steep, scree slopes. From Hoover Lakes, you are about five miles from Green Creek, TH55, which would make an 11-mile car-shuttle hike, and avoid having to hump back up Summit Lake Saddle.

BP: An excellent trailhead with several options. Summit Lake is one possible direction for a 3- to 5-night car-shuttle trip ending up at Lembert Dome in Tuolumne Meadows, TH61. Hoover Lakes is a direction for a shorter car-shuttle trip, with the second car at Green Creek, TH55. You can also reach the Green Creek trailhead by taking the Virginia Canyon trail north from the west end of Summit Lake, which leads over Virginia Pass and comes down Glines Canyon. Cooney and Frog Lakes are first-night flops for late-arriving packers, or destination lakes for trips with kids.

B: Virginia Lakes are good-sized, high-elevation lakes with easy access, in the shadow of mountains. Sleeper kayak and canoe destination.

F: **Virginia Lakes** lend themselves to small craft fishing, float tubes and shore casting. Lake fly-fishermen, in search or rainbow and cutthroat, may want to walk to **Cooney Lake** and **Frog Lakes**.

57. MONO LAKE H, MB, B

Best for: Rock hounds, geologists, photographers, mountain bikers, kayakers, and short hikes on driving tour.

Park: Take Hwy. 395 to 5 mi. south of Lee Vining, turn east on Hwy. 120 and follow signs to south tufas and Panum Crater.

Map: Mono Craters

H: Panum Crater and south tufas, 1 to 3 mi., 300 ft.; Mono Craters, 2 mi., 1000 ft.

A .5-mile walk gets you to large, obsidian-and-pumice strewn **Panum Crater**, its rim affording a panorama of Mono Lake. You can walk quite a bit more around the crater, and more still into it. The obsidian in this crater was the primary trading commodity for the local Paiute Indians. Arrowheads and chips found in Alpine County likely came from this locale. Heed posted signs prohibiting removal of rock samples. *Watch out:* Sharp rocks and bad footing await if straying too far from trails. Travelling off-trail across Panum Crater is not recommended.

A short drive from Panum Crater, to the lakeshore leads to the eerily beautiful **South Tufas**. You can roam around the spires and also take off on longer hikes along the shoreline in either direction. West of the tufas is where Rush Creek runs through Pumice Valley and refreshes Mono Lake with snowmelt. This creek is the main contributor to the lake.

Then get back in the car and go east on Hwy. 120 for 5 miles, up to the **Mono Craters** turnout. From Crater Mountain is a remarkable and seldom photographed view of the lake. A trail leads from the roadside to the crater rims.

MB: Mono Lake is encircled by a number of dirt and sand roads, which see few cars. On the north and east shores, roads are too soft, and even mountain bikers may have to escort their wheels here and there. High brush and dunes can get you lost on the far shores of the lake, so be careful.

B: Kayaking or canoeing around the tufas and islands of Mono Lake is high on a list of good experiences. Check with ranger to determine off-limit island boundaries. *Watch out:* Don't let wind or lightning catch you too far from shore.

58. MONO PASS   H, BP, CC, F

Best for:	Tibetan-like grandeur, sleeper Yosemite backpack, glimpse at Ansel Adams Wilderness with wildflowers and old-growth conifers along the way.
Park:	On Hwy. 120, 2 mi. west of Tioga Pass entrance to Yosemite. Look for parking area on left (south) side of road. At 9700 ft.
Maps:	Tuolumne Meadows and Mono Craters

Mono Lake

H: Dana Meadows, 3 mi., no elevation; Mono Pass only, 7 mi., 900 ft.; Parker Pass only, 11 mi., 1400 ft.; Helen Lake loop, 13 mi. (2.5 mi. off-trail), 1700 ft. *Note:* Option to shorten loop hike by 2 mi. and 400 ft. by not going to lake.

To **Mono Pass**, the route of the ancients through the mountains, head south through **Dana Meadows**. The trail crosses the Dana Fork of the Tuolumne River less than a mile from the trailhead. You can wander the river on either side of the trail, coming upon lakelets, pools and a wide variety of wildflowers.

To continue to Mono Pass, stay on the trail southbound—it will join but not cross Parker Pass Creek in about two miles. In another mile, bear left—east and up—at the Parker Creek trail junction. You'll come to the Mono Pass trail—you can walk in-and-out to Mono Pass for the view and then continue to Parker Pass.

To **Parker Pass**, continue south at the junction with Mono Pass trail. You'll pass sheepherder's abandoned stone cabins, below which is a large cataract gushing over marbled bedrock. Continuing down another couple hundred feet, and east, you reach the outer edge of the Ansel Adams Wilderness, at Parker Pass, with its steep, stark formations and east Sierra views.

To **return, via Kuna Ridge lakes**, including **Helen Lake**, backtrack one mile, passing the trail you walked in on and heading toward Spillway Lake. From Spillway Lake, you can follow the creek which fills the lake's southern end, off-trail and up to Helen Lake. From Helen Lake, contour north to Bingaman and Kuna Lakes, which are held in the basins of rugged Kuna Ridge. From Kuna Lake, drop down northeasterly to join the return trail.

For an easier **return via Parker Pass Creek,** take the trail that leads out of the north end of Spillway Lake, paralleling Kuna Ridge, but several hundred feet below it.

BP: Dana Meadows is a little used, close-to-the-car backpack stop. Parker Pass has many backpack sites, with dwarf whitebark pine to provide shelter.

CC: In the winter when Tioga Pass is closed, Nordic skiers drive up the road as far as possible and ski in toward Tuolumne Meadows. Tioga Lodge, at the top of Hwy. 120 just before you enter the park, stays open in the winter to accommodate skiers, with snowmobile service that puts you at the gateway to Tuolumne Meadows and its miles of open skiing.

F: The Dana Fork of the Tuolumne River, which you reach less than a mile from the trailhead, is not visited by many anglers, and therefore a likely place to fly-cast for trout. Lake fishermen try **Tioga Lake**, on the road just at the top of Tioga Pass. East of Tioga Pass, along the several-mile, fairly flat section of Hwy. 120 as you turn up from Hwy. 395, are several roads into to campgrounds along **Lee Vining Creek**, a good region to fly-fish. Along Lee Vining Creek are several forest service campgrounds set within resplendent aspen groves.

59. GAYLOR LAKES H, BP

Best for: Frozen lakes, clear brooks, lawn-like flower garden, mine ruins.

Park: On Hwy. 120, at Gaylor Lakes Creek, 4.5 mi. west of Tioga Pass entrance to Yosemite. On west side of creek as it passes under road. At 9200 ft.

Map: Tuolumne Meadows

H: Lower Gaylor Lake, 4.5 mi., 900 ft.; Middle Gaylor, 7 mi. (3 mi. off-trail), 1200 ft.; Upper Gaylor, 8 mi., (3 off-trail), 1500 ft.; Great Sierra Mine, 10 mi., (3 mi. off-trail), 1700 ft.; Granite Lakes, 10.5 mi. (3.5 off-trail), 1700 ft. *Note:* All off-trail is easy.

To **Lower Gaylor Lake,** walk the trail up the west side of the creek through lodgepole, heading north, and then veering away from the creek. After about 1.5 miles, you'll come out into the green, high-altitude slope to the lake.

To **Middle Gaylor Lake,** go off-trail to the northeast, over lawn-like terrain dotted with dwarf wildflowers and a capillary system of brooklets.

To **Upper Gaylor Lake,** find the trail that runs along the north side of creek that feeds Middle Gaylor from the north, and follow it up to the last Gaylor. This trail comes in from Tioga Pass.

To **Great Sierra Mine** ruins (stone cabin), proceed north on a trail up west shore of Upper Gaylor. To **Granite Lakes**—two of them—drop back down to Upper Gaylor, and contour due west. These high lakes are often still frozen aquamarine in summer, their surfaces creaking and snapping as they thaw. To return, follow the drainage south out of lower Granite Lake.

Note: Lower Gaylor is filled by the drainage of Granite Lakes, not by the other Gaylor lakes.

BP: This area sees a fair number day hikers, but not many backpackers. Suitable for short-duration trips.

60. LYELL CANYON H, BP

Best for: Miles without elevation gain, glacier-water rivers, flowers and big pines, organized pack trips.

Park: Enter Yosemite via Tioga Pass entrance off Hwy. 395. Go 6 mi. to Tuolumne Meadows High Sierra Camp road, trailhead parking just east of ranger station. At 8700 ft.

Map: Tuolumne Meadows

H: Tuolumne River Bridges, 2 mi., 150 ft.; Vogelsang High Sierra Camp via Rafferty Creek, 13 mi., 1400 ft.; Lyell Canyon, 12 to 16 mi., 300 ft.

To **Vogelsang High Sierra Camp**, take the trail that forks right, south, about .5-mile from the awe-inspiring **bridges over the Tuolumne River**, which are about a mile from the trailhead. You'll ascend gradually through lodgepole forest, skirting Rafferty Creek, until staircasing up to seemingly landscaped meadowlands on the approach to Vogelsang High Sierra Camp. There, enjoy a lemonade from the camp kitchen at the cascade under towering peaks, making sure marmots don't get your lunch. *Note:* You can walk back via Evelyn Lake and Lyell Canyon, but this makes for a 22-mile day.

To **Lyell Canyon,** once home to the longest glacier in the world, is a flat walk along granitoid Tuolumne River. After taking the left fork beyond the above-mentioned bridges, the trail is flat along the meadow for about 8 miles, with Kuna Ridge on one side and several large peaks on the other. About 7 miles in you'll get view of Donahue Pass, up which many backpackers make a pilgrimage each year.

Vogelsang High Sierra Camp

Note: Another, seldom used trail up Lyell Canyon lies on the other, east, side of the river. On this trail, you will come across two spots with lakelets and pools both right on the river. One spot is about 5 miles in from the trailhead, and the other is about 7 miles in. Be aware that the frigid and deep waters make the Lyell Fork of the Tuolumne difficult to cross, so don't count on a loop hike.

BP: Many people and bears frequent these trails. Donahue Pass round-trip makes a good 3-day excursion, with a base camp 8 miles in, on the north side of Donahue. The pass, with an active glacier nearby, is a magnet for hikers from all over the world. Another backpacking option—which requires a car-shuttle—is to continue south over Donahue into the Thousand Island Lakes basin, coming out eventually at Reds Meadow in Mammoth Lakes. For a loop trip, try the Evelyn Lake Trail, which goes west midway up Lyell Canyon. You'll come back Rafferty Creek via Vogelsang High Sierra Camp as per hiking description above.

Watch out: Bears are known to frequent campsites, especially popular ones. One packers campground above upper Lyell Meadow has bear cables and boxes. If you camp away from people you are less likely to be visited by a bear.

61. LOWER TUOLUMNE H, BP, CC

Best for: Viewing one of the world's grandest stretches of falling white water, backpack destinations, horseback trips.

Park: From Tioga Pass entrance, go west 10 mi. on Hwy. 120, to Lembert Dome Picnic area on right. Glen Aulin hikes, drive in .5-mi. to trailhead parking at stables. At 8800 ft.

Map: Tuolumne Meadows

H: Glen Aulin, 11 mi., 900 ft.; California Falls, 15 mi., 1300 ft.; Waterwheel Falls, 18 mi., 2100 ft. *Note:* Shorter hikes anywhere along the river.

Glenn Aulin High Sierra Camp is down the Tuolumne River, on a trail winding its way through the serene meadows with views to the south—peaks tufted like meringue due to glacial scouring. Hikers wishing to go shorter distances can get to dramatic spots on the river after a couple of miles. Just above Glen Aulin you come to Tuolumne Falls, beginning a 6-mile run of falls, cascades and pools as the river drops toward the Grand Canyon of the Tuolumne River. Glen Aulin has large pool and cascade falling through reddish rock amphitheater.

Keep going, as energy permits, down to **California** and **Le Conte Falls**, just above **Waterwheel**—which is named for its shooting roostertails of water.

Watch out: This is all a downhill from the trailhead; though it is high-speed trail, you could wind up on a longer hike that you realize.

BP: Backpacker camp at Glen Aulin, with many day-hike options from there. This trailhead is also a good southern terminus for 3- to 5-night pack trips that begin at Twin Lakes, TH54, or Virginia Lakes, TH56. Packers can also head down-river from Glen Aulin passing the falls noted above, through the Grand Canyon of the Tuolumne River and into Hetch Hetchy Valley.

Note: A backpackers' campground at Glen Aulin has bear boxes and cables.

CC: Many people snow camp in Tuolumne Meadows, after getting snowmobiles rides as far as possible up Tioga Road. Tioga Lodge, a private concern a couple miles east of the park entrance, caters to Nordic skiers.

62. LEMBERT DOME H, BP

  Best for: Tuolumne Meadows overlook, high lakes surrounded by granite monoliths.
    Park: From Tioga Pass entrance, go west 10 mi. on Hwy. 120, to Lembert Dome Picnic area on right. At 8800 ft.
    Map: Tuolumne Meadows

H: Lembert Dome, 4 mi., 600 ft.; Dog Lake, 3.5 mi., 500 ft.; Young Lakes loop, 17 mi., 1900 ft.; Soda Springs, 1.5 mi., 150 ft.

The **Lembert Dome** trail is along the west side of the big rock, hiking north, and then turning east around the back of it. Once around back, the walk up is easy. There are many possible routes going down—you can walk down the granite on the east side, traversing away from the picnic area as you descend.

Watch out: Those granite ramps can turn too steep imperceptibly as you go down and put you on your face. Also what is easily scrambled up can be too steep to come down.

To **Dog Lake,** one of Tuolumne's larger lakes, look for a trail on the right, .25-mile beyond the Lembert Dome trail turnoff, and walk in about .5-mile.

To **Young Lakes,** start out on the Lembert trail, but pass options to the dome and Dog Lake, and continue north. You'll cross Delaney and then Dingley Creek, before reaching a trail junction that takes you the last 2.3 miles around Ragged Peak to Lower Young Lake (there are three lakes, west to east). Young Lakes sit below a skyscraper ridge and affords big views toward Roosevelt Lake and northern Yosemite. To get back, take the right, easterly, junction at the trail 2.3 miles from Young Lakes. Follow that trail south 3.9 miles, crossing Dingley Creek again, further downstream, and meeting up with the Glen Aulin trail back to the stables.

Take this trail left, east, back to Lembert via Soda Springs. **Soda Springs**, bubbling naturally carbonated mineral water, is near Parsons Lodge, a historic stone building. This is also a sunny picnic spot—go down the trail into the meadow from the stables.

BP: Backpacker's might want to spend several nights day hiking around Young Lakes. Plenty of hard rock for climbers.

Watch out: Although bears aren't as common here as some lower elevation Yosemite camping areas, don't be surprised to have one come calling; hang food. Rangers at the Tuolumne wilderness permit registration booth and Tuolumne Store rent bear-proof cannisters that will fit in your backpack.

63.   TENAYA LAKE   H, BP, B, F

Best for:	Scaling Half Dome's famous sidekick without driving into Yosemite Valley.
Park:	From Yosemite National Park east entrance, go about 17 mi. to Tenaya Lake. Park at west end of lake. At 8500 ft.
Map:	Hetch Hetchy Reservoir

H: Clouds Rest, 14 mi., 1700 ft.

Clouds Rest is a no-hands climb. From Tenaya Lake, the trail leads past Sunrise Pass, through a towering fir and pine forest. You continue through the forested south side of the mountain, until the final several hundred feet of upping, when you take gradual switchbacks to the top. The top of Clouds Rest, which in fact does tend to collect cloud shreds from the valley, is a .25-mile long, 15-foot wide granite spine that is Tenaya Creek's south face. Half Dome is about 2.5 air miles to the southwest of Clouds Rest, with Quarter Dome in between.

Note: Clouds Rest is the eastern-most and has the highest elevation among the peaks that can be seen from Yosemite Valley.

BP: Plenty of people take this route to Clouds Rest and Half Dome, but it is far less used than the trail up from Yosemite Valley. You can walk Clouds Rest on day one, set up camp nearby, and do Half Dome (a must-do experience at some point in one's life) the next day. Water could be a problem: It's available a couple hundred feet below and slightly east the junction of the Half Dome Trail from Little Yosemite Valley, or at a reliable spring a mile up toward Half Dome from that junction.

B: From the middle of Tenaya Lake in a canoe or kayak, you are in the center of a polished granite stadium. A rose-colored alpenglow sunset can be particularly beautiful.

F: Float tubers and kayak fishermen test their luck in **Tenaya Lake.** The creeks of **Tuolumne Meadows** are also fishable. Other fishermen try **Tioga Lake** and **Ellery Lake,** which are on Hwy. 120, on the east side of the park entrance.

64. MAY LAKE H, BP, F

Best for:	Getting to a four-star peak, wildflowers along the way.
Park:	From Yosemite National Park east entrance, go about 17 mi. to 3.5 mi. west of Tenaya Lake. Turn right, north, toward May Lake, another 2 mi. At 8800 ft.
Maps:	Tuolumne Meadows and Hetch Hetchy

H: May Lake, 3.5 mi., 500 ft.; Polly Dome Lakes, 12 mi., 800 ft.; Glen Aulin bus-shuttle, 16 mi., 1500 ft.; Mount Hoffman, 7.5 mi., 2100 ft.

May Lake is one of five High Sierra Camps that encircle the greater Tuolumne Meadows. To some, May Lake is a particular favorite as it affords a faraway feel, yet is only about three miles from the main highway. Tent cabin accommodations and a community dining tent located on the lakeshore make this camp so popular it can take years to obtain a reservation. The camps have been operating since the late 1920s.

For the **Glen Aulin bus-shuttle**, a trail leads north from May Lake, eight miles to the High Sierra Camp at Glen Aulin. About three miles from May Lake on this trail, look for the trail on the right that jogs to **Polly Dome Lake**s which are an interesting destination for an option to the bus-shuttle hike.

From Glen Aulin, it is a five-mile walk out to Lembert Dome. A regularly scheduled shuttle bus runs through Tuolumne Meadows back to the May Lake trailhead—a trailhead on the highway, not the one you can drive to described in the parking directions. Confirm shuttle-bus hours of operation at Tuolumne Meadows Visitor Center.

Clouds Rest

Mount Hoffman is not visible behind the peak that rises above May Lake. The trail to Mount Hoffman leaves via the southern shore of May Lake and climbs through a series of cataracts and meadows. Bogs of lush green vegetation are accented with dark blue clumps of lupine. It then switchbacks northerly, giving you views of Cathedral Peak and other peaks to the south. Then you reach a sweeping bowl that leads the final six or seven hundred feet to the top—toward your left, or west. The last bit is a doable rock climb, leading to one of the most beautiful vistas in the Sierra.

Note: Mount Hoffman is at the geographic center of Yosemite National Park.

BP: Like all Tuolumne packers' camps, May Lake is used by many people, especially since it is close to the road. You may wish to check out unofficial campsites at the northeast shore, perhaps using bear cables at the regular site.

F: Hikers willing to walk in with a fly-casting pole may hook a rainbow trout dinner from the depths of **May Lake**.

Tahoe

Upper Truckee River

Lake Tahoe holds enough water to deluge the entire state of California more than a foot deep. But not a drop actually gets there. The Tahoe Basin all drains northeast, via the Truckee River, through Reno and into Pyramid Lake.

Desolation Wilderness, holding dozens of granite lakes above the lake's southwest shore, is one of California's most popular hiking regions. The Fallen Leaf, upper Emerald Bay and Echo Lakes portions of Desolation drain back into Tahoe. Desolation's more westerly portion, around Lake Aloha, empties into Horsetail Falls and the American River, eventually finding salt water in the San Francisco Bay.

The southern Tahoe Rim is formed by Alpine's bulwark of peaks—Red Lake, Stevens, Thompson, Jobs Sister, and Freel. At 10,881 feet, Freel Peak is the highest point in the Tahoe Basin.

The first European making record of seeing Lake Tahoe was General John Fremont in 1844, from atop Stevens Peak or Red Lake Peak—accounts differ—after having come through the East Carson Canyon. Five years later Fremont was back in Washington D.C. as a nominee for President of the United States, and thousands of California-bound gold seekers beheld the vast blue waters.

Many different names were tried for the lake, including Lake Bonpland after Fremont's botanist and Lake Bigler after California's governor. But "Tahoe" stuck. It's the English spelling of the Washo word, "Dah'-Ho," meaning "Big Water." No place name is more appropriate. The Washo Indians used the sandy south shore of the lake for their summer Gumsaba, or "Big Time," when one of three main tribes gathered and took whitefish in celebration of the season's plenty.

During three seasons of the year, the Washo foraged the Sierra knowing specifically where and when to go given the weather pattern of a particular year. In the winter, they headed down to the piñon pines and hot springs of eastern Alpine.

The Gold Rush emigrants shook the Washo world. But Tahoe's real awakening didn't happen until 1860 when the Comstock Lode erupted in Virginia City and the lake's fish and timber were greatly depleted.

By the turn of the century, the boom days were over. The early 1900s saw huge mansions and lodges around the lakeshore—some of which are preserved at Baldwin Beach—serviced by lake ferries and the railroad from San Francisco. Tahoe was quite the destination for the leisure class.

By the 1960s and 70s, tourism developed into casinos and full-on growth, which threatened the clarity of the lake's waters. But the formation of the Tahoe Regional Planning Agency and League to Save Lake Tahoe have been successful in curbing growth and improving water quality. Unfortunately, recent studies have shown much lake pollution is airborne, coming in over the Sierra from northern California.

Although Tahoe is quite developed, it still offers easy access to exceptional backcountry and water-sport recreation. And it remains, to paraphrase Mark Twain, surely among the fairest pictures the whole earth affords.

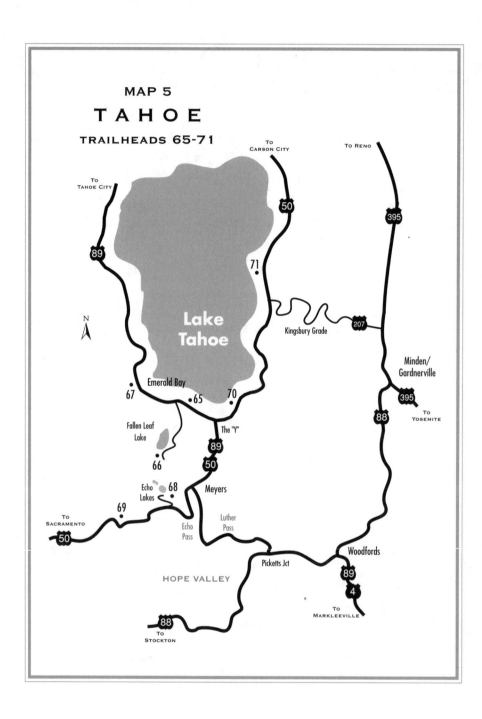

MAP 5

TAHOE

TRAILHEADS 65-71

To Tahoe City

To Carson City

To Reno

89

50

395

71

Kingsbury Grade

207

Lake Tahoe

Minden/ Gardnerville

Emerald Bay

67

65

70

395

Fallen Leaf Lake

The "Y"

88

89

To Yosemite

50

66

Echo Lakes

68

Meyers

69

Luther Pass

To Sacramento

Echo Pass

Woodfords

50

Picketts Jct

89

HOPE VALLEY

4

To Markleeville

88

To Stockton

N

TAHOE
TRAILHEAD DESCRIPTIONS

TRAILHEADS 65–71
MAP 5

H=Day Hiking, BP=Backpacking, MB=Mountain Biking,
CC=Cross Country Skiing, B=Boating, F=Fishing

65. KIVA BEACH WALK H, MB, B

Best for: Fall color walk along lakeshore, summer swimming, tour of old Tahoe
mansions, picnic, bike ride.

Park: From the "Y" at South Lake Tahoe, jct. Hwys. 50/89, take Hwy 89
north about 4 mi., passing Camp Richardson. Turn right at Tallac
Historic Site, a park road, and then veer left to Kiva Beach lot.

Map: Fallen Leaf Lake

H: Kiva and Baldwin beach, and Tallac Historic Site walks, 0 to 3 mi., no elevation.

Kiva Beach, a short walk from the lot, is a spit of sand separating Lake Tahoe from the
Taylor Creek marsh, with its eagle habitat and rainbow trout migratory waters. Warm,
shallow water of Tahoe here, and view of Mount Tallac, make for outstanding summer
swimming.

You can walk and wade the shore westward toward **Baldwin Beach**. Or head east along a
footpath to the **Tallac Historic Site,** a first-class park preserving the mansions of the late
1800s. Included are the remnants of Lucky Baldwin's Tallac House and Tallac Casino, and
the grounds of the Pope and Valhalla estates. Peek through the windows of the restored
cottages for a view of what it was like to be a summer guest. The Tallac site hosts a number
of events including the Washo Tribe summer gathering and several art festivals. A Lakeside
restaurant with a dock open to visitors is a few hundred feet east along the water from the
Tallac grounds.

At the **Visitors Center**, a .5-mile or less walk westward from the Kiva lot through lodge-pole pine (or drive on Hwy. 89 to the next turnoff) is a self-guided tour of aspen-laden **Taylor Creek.** Follow the signs to a building which houses an underwater viewing area of the stream's several species of fish. Children will love it. Big fat trout pose for photographs behind glass in a submerged streambed diorama.

Local lore: Melting snow on the east face Mt. Tallac forms a "cross" in the late spring and summer. Washo legend says if this cross melts through in any section before July—when their summer Gumsaba, or "Big Time" took place—a harsh winter will follow.

MB: Bike trails run along the highway, beginning before Richardsons Bay, and also through the Tallac Historic Site, continuing to where the road twists and climbs toward Emerald Bay. The area is made for exploring by bike. Several bike rental companies are located along the strip of highway that extends from the the "Y" to Richardsons Bay.

B: You'll have to carry the canoe or kayak a couple hundred feet to the water, but the shallow water keeps power boats away and is ideal for paddlers.

Moonlight on Lake Tahoe

66. FALLEN LEAF LAKE   H, BP, MB, CC, B, F

Best for: Day hiking, fall backpacking, wildflowers, lakes galore,
spectacular Tahoe view, jumping into cold water.

Park: From the "Y" at South Lake Tahoe, jct. Hwys. 50/89, take Hwy. 89
for about 5 mi. to the Fallen Leaf Lake turnoff, on the left. Go in
5 mi., passing marina and winding up the last 1.5 mi. to a paved
parking area. At 6700 ft. For Angora Lake, park near lake at entrance
to Stanford Camp road.

Map: Fallen Leaf Lake

H: Glen Alpine falls, 1.5 mi., 200 ft.; Grass Lake, 5 mi., 800 ft.; Susie Lake, 8 mi.,
1100 ft.; Gilmore Lake, 10 mi., 1700 ft.; Mt. Tallac, 14 mi., 3000 ft.; Dicks
Pass, 14 mi., 2500 ft.; Dicks Peak, 16 mi. (2 mi. off-trail), 3300 ft.; Triangle
Lake, 5.5 mi., 1300 ft.; Echo Peak, 6.5 mi. (2 miles off-trail), 2300 ft.; Angora
Lakes, 3 mi., 900ft.

The trail to **Grass Lake** is a left fork, about .5-mile after the rustic structures at **Glen
Alpine Falls**. To get to **Susie Lake,** pass the Grass Lake fork, continue 1 mile, and take a
fork to the left (west). To **Gilmore Lake,** bypass the trail(s) to Susie Lake, and one to Half
Moon Lake, and follow signs to a trail that switchbacks up and northerly. Gilmore sits in
a large basin below Mt. Tallac.

From Gilmore Lake, **Mt. Tallac** is a 2-mile, 1300-foot scamper through a zone rich in
flowers. At the top are breathtaking vistas of the Tahoe Basin. Hikers with sturdy knees
can make Mt. Tallac a loop hike by taking the Cathedral Lake trail back to Fallen Leaf—
the trail takes off to the east, beginning .25-mile from the south of the peak. When you
get to Fallen Leaf Lake on this trail, look for rocks where locals take the plunge into cold
water.

Dicks Pass, a vantage point for the many lakes of the Rockbound Valley above Emerald
Bay, is achieved by taking the trail that forks to the left, less than .25-mile south on your
approach to Gilmore Lake. To **Dicks Peak,** an exhausting but rewarding day hike, leave
the trail at Dicks Pass, heading due west up the steep shoulder of the mountain.

The trail to **Triangle Lake** takes off to the left, on the east side of Lily Lake just as you
leave the trailhead. Slack water and brush can make it hard to find—stay to the east of the
cabins. You climb steeply through boulders and bush, below the east face of Indian Rock.
The trail pops out at a flat, open saddle from where a short trail jogs north to tiny Triangle
Lake. To **Echo Peak**—which affords a spot-on look at Echo Lakes—walk east from the
saddle, making sure to stay clear of brush on the peak's south face.

To **Angora Lakes**—which you can also drive to—take a trail beginning on the south side of the creek at the trailhead. The trail switchbacks easterly and steeply, before joining the rough road that comes into the lakes. Angora Lakes are postcard-quality, with summer cabins and steep walls rising on three sides.

Watch out: Trails can be confusing in Desolation Wilderness, so check your map and follow signs. Off-trail walking is made difficult by small rocks, rock sub-formations and pesky manzanita and other brush. Definitely not a place for as-the-crow-flies hiking.

BP: Desolation Wilderness is a backpacker's paradise, made less so only by its popularity. Lake basins and rumpled topography provide many campsites.

MB: The paved road to Fallen Leaf is a dicey ride, due to traffic on summer weekends, but very scenic on any day. Before the Fallen Leaf Road narrows, and continues to the cabins and Stanford Camp, you can veer off along the lake's southern shore. You'll connect with other roads that lead to a north trailhead to Mt. Tallac.

CC: Park at the highway and ski in on the road through the (closed) campground to Fallen Leaf Lake. A second road skirts partway on the lake's western shore.

B: Kayaking, canoeing and sailing are all popular at Fallen Leaf Lake. A paddle around the entire shoreline would be about eight miles.

F: **Gilmore Lake**, with a variety of fish, including Kamloops, big browns and mackinaw, is a favorite lake among hike-in fishermen. **Cathedral Lake**, a short but steep hike from the west shore of Fallen Leaf, is one of the more accessible places to try for golden trout.

67. EMERALD BAY H, BP, B, F

Best for: Vikingsholm, granite lakes, day hike with dinner at Tahoe.

Park: From the "Y" at South Lake Tahoe, jct. Hwys. 50/89, take Hwy. 89 about 9 mi. to Emerald Bay. Lot for lake hikes is on left, the Eagle Falls trailhead; Vikingsholm lot is less than .25 mi. past that, on right. For Granite Lake park at the Bay View Campground, 1 mi. east of Eagle Falls parking. For Eagle Point, park at Eagle Point Campground, 1.5 mi. east of Eagle Falls. At 6600 ft.

Map: Fallen Leaf

H: Vikingsholm, 1 mi., 400 ft.; Emerald Point, 4.5 mi., 400 ft.; Fontanillis Lake, Dicks Lake and Velma Lakes loop, 10 mi. (2 mi. off trail), 1900 ft.; Granite Lake, 2 mi., 800 ft.; Eagle Point, 1 mi., 200 ft.

Vikingsholm, a Norseman's castle/home now restored as a park, sits on the sandy shore of Emerald Bay. This is one of the Sierra's most beautiful spots—don't let crowds turn you off. Walking the grounds and seeing Emerald Bay from lake-level is especially pleasant during the quieter times, late spring and early fall. Tours are offered during the summer. To **Emerald Point**, which is the west side of the mouth of Emerald Bay, walk toward Tahoe on the north side of the bay. You can follow a road at first and then, passing cabins, make your way along a shoreline trail.

For the **lakes loop hike**, beginning at the Eagle Falls parking, start up the rock staircase, crossing the footbridge at **Eagle Falls**. **Dicks Lake** is reached after climbing a rocky ramp and navigating a couple different drainages; follow signs. From Dicks to **Fontanillis Lake**, don't take the trail southward toward Dicks Pass—rather, go on an easy off-trail jaunt to the northwest, reaching the ameba-shaped Fontanillis—which is filled by Dicks drainage.

Upper Velma Lake—and the trail—is .5-mile down from Fontanillis Lake, from its north end. The trail loops within range, but not quite to **Middle and Lower Velma lakes**, before rejoining the trail you came in on. To get to those two lakes, jump off the main trail; just make sure to come back to the east, and not the trail taking you further west into Desolation Wilderness.

To **Granite Lake** from the Bay View parking area, take the trail from the back end of the campground loop road. You will switchback at the outset, and then climb less steeply until reaching the small but scenic lake. *Note:* This trail continues, ascending, and meets up with the trail headed toward Dicks Lake from Eagle Falls.

Eagle Point forms the east side of the opening to Emerald Bay. Parking at the campground may be difficult on summer days, and a day-use fee may apply. The short walk is down to a dramatic perch above the bay.

BP: This zone is popular among packers for good reason: it's great packing with numerous lakeside camp spots and day-hike options.

B: Emerald Bay, with its island and remote shoreline that is part of Bliss State Park, is an exotic kayaking and canoeing destination. People camp without fires along this shoreline in spots accessible only from the water. You can't put in here, since the road is several hundred feet above the water. Baldwin Beach is one good launching spot to explore Emerald Bay.

F: Fishermen may want to hike directly, 5 miles one-way, to **Middle Velma Lake** for good-sized rainbows.

68. ECHO LAKES H, BP, CC, B, F

Best for: Summer cabin resort, entrance to land of lakes and polished granite, lake-dipping and sun drying.

Park: Take Echo Lakes/Berkeley Camp Road off Hwy. 50, 4 mi. west of jct. Hwys. 89/50 in Meyers. Drive in 2.5 mi. to marina lot, or park at overflow higher up. At 7400 ft. For car-shuttle, park second car at Horsetail Falls, TH69.

Map: Fallen Leaf Lake

H: Lake Aloha, Desolation Wilderness, 14 mi., 900 ft.; Pyramid Peak, 16 mi. (6 mi. off-trail), 2400 ft.; Echo Lake to Horsetail Falls car-shuttle, 11 mi., 1000 ft.

The walk to **Lake Aloha** can be shortened by 4 or 5 miles—and made more fun—by taking the boat taxi from the marina at Lower Echo. The taxi shuttles hikers to Upper Echo Lake. The trail from lower Echo runs along the north shore behind cabins of Echo Lakes and then becomes a rocky ramp all the way to Aloha.

Many side trips are possible—Ralston Lake, Tamarack Lake, Lake LeConte, Triangle Lake, Lake of the Woods, Lake Margery, and Lake Lucille.

You'll see several of these lakes from the trail including Tamarack, Margery and LeConte. Triangle Lake is described in the Fallen Leaf hikes, TH66; a hike from Echo Lakes to Fallen Leaf via Triangle Lake would be a six-mile car shuttle, utilizing the boat taxi.

For **Echo Lake to Horsetail car-shuttle**, take a trail to the south, about 1 mile before reaching Lake Aloha, and just before passing Lake Margery. This trail continues along the east shore of Lake of the Woods and down the east side of Horsetail Falls.

To scale **Pyramid Peak**, the sentinel of the Tahoe Sierra and American River drainage, leave the trail, heading due west, just as you get to the south end of Lake Aloha. Make your way through the numerous small lakes, keeping Pyramid to your right, or north. Start to climb, still heading west, until Pyramid is directly north, and climb that shoulder—the peak's south face—to the top.

BP: With so many visitors, Desolation can seem more a park than a wilderness, but enough lakes abound to find a spot of your own.

CC: The road into Echo Lakes is a 4- or 5-mile round-trip run. Echo Lakes are quite a sight in winter, frozen and buried in snow.

B: Classic canoeing and kayaking, though water skiers make waves. Check out the channel between Upper and Lower Echo. The islets of Upper Echo make for paddle-and-camp destinations.

Desolation Wilderness

F: **Desolation Wilderness** is stocked with virtually all mountain trout: golden, rainbow, brown, brook, mackinaw and cutthroat. In the area of Lake Aloha, some good bets for hike-in fishermen are **Tamarack Lake, Lake Lucille, Lake Margery** and **Heather Lake**. In Echo Lakes, with a boat ramp accessible by car, you can also catch fat Kokanee Salmon, a species planted in the 1940s.

69.   HORSETAIL FALLS H, BP

    Best for: Falls view, back door to Desolation Wilderness and swimming lakes.
    Park: At Twin Bridges on Hwy. 50, 7 mi. west of Echo Summit. At 6000 ft.
    Map: Fallen Leaf Lake

H: Horsetail Falls top and Avalanche Lake, 4 mi., 1300 ft.; Lake of the Woods, 8 mi., 1900 ft.; Lake Aloha, 10 mi., 2000 ft.

Horsetail Falls, the spewing of Pyramid Creek as it drains Lake Aloha and about a dozen smaller lakes from Desolation Valley, is a short and breathtaking hike. Be sure to stay on trail to avoid impassible alder and brush.

At the top is **Avalanche Lake**, one of more than a dozen lakes and lakelets which dot the mile-square granite zone southwest of lake Aloha—an interesting area to explore, provided you keep your bearings. To **Lake of the Woods**, take a trail heading northwest from Avalanche Lake. The Aloha trail runs along the north shore of Lake of the Woods, which you can take and then loop back to the trail down Horsetail Falls.

BP: Horsetail Falls is a good exit point for car-shuttle pack trips that begin at Echo Lakes, TH68, or Fallen Leaf Lake, TH66. Not many people choose to start here and march up with a heavy pack.

70.   TRUCKEE MARSH H, MB, B, F

    Best for: Bird-watching beach stroll, sandy swimming and kayaking.
    Park: Turn left, north, on Tahoe Keys Blvd. off Hwy. 50, 1.5 mi. east of the "Y," jct. Hwys. 50/89. Go 1 mi., turn right on Venice Blvd. Park at trailhead across from marina.
    Map: Freel Peak

H: Tahoe at Truckee Marsh, 1.5 mi., no elevation.

Walk the **Truckee Marsh**—where the Truckee River spreads out among willows as it fills Lake Tahoe—and keep an eye out for waterfowl, blue heron and eagles. This short walk is perfect for sunset or sunrise. You can walk and wade the sandy shore for a quarter-mile or so in either direction.

MB: Ride out to the water, or take roads through Tahoe Keys houses, skirting the lakeshore, and come out on Hwy. 89 to pick up the bike path to Kiva Beach and Tallac area.

B: Marina at Tahoe Keys is set up for full-scale boat launches. Canoeists and kayakers can also put in here and paddle the channels among lake-front homes, or take the main channel out into Tahoe. Hope Valley Outdoor Center rents kayaks here.

F: In **Lake Tahoe** are huge fish swimming up to several hundred feet deep. Boat fishermen take off from Tahoe Keys Marina, as well as Zephyr Cove, north of Nevada Beach, Carnelian Bay on the north shore. Contact the visitors center or Tahoe Chamber for more fishing information.

71. NEVADA BEACH WALK   H, B

Best for:	Swimming, dog swimming, star gazing, off-season beach walks.
Park:	Turn left (west) toward Nevada Beach, off Hwy. 50, 1.5 mi. north of jct. Hwy. 50 and Kingsbury Grade, Hwy. 207. Fee parking inside park —when park is open during summer and fall—or street parking just outside of gate. At 6200 ft.
Map:	Freel Peak

H: Nevada Beach 1 to 3 mi., no elevation.

At **Nevada Beach**, large Jeffrey pines spaced in granite sand lead to the blue waters of Tahoe and an in-your-face look at the lake's western peaks. The walk north is short, ending at the boathouse at Marla Bay. The walk south passes several docks, along the golf course and beyond the Edgewood Country Club. To get to the dog beach, leash your pet and walk south on paved roads through the campground until roads end at a Nevada State boat park. In all seasons but summer, Nevada Beach is used by few people.

Note: Signs notwithstanding, it is lawful to walk the entire shoreline of Lake Tahoe, as long as you stay at water's edge, or within the lake's high-water shore.

B: The best canoeing and kayaking is north from Nevada Beach, toward Marla Bay, Zephyr Cove and the remote beaches on Tahoe's northeast shore.

DRIVING TOURS
Sights and regional history

TOUR 1
EMIGRANT HIGH COUNTRY

*Along portions of the Emigrant Trail, Pony Express route and Snowshoe
Thompson's tracks, into the high valleys of the Carson Pass.*

Approximate time: 2 to 3 hours.

START AT WOODFORDS, JCT. HWYS. 88/89.

In 1847, Samuel Brannan renamed a sacred Washo falls that gushed from a mountain
high above after himself. Brannan Springs became a way station for Mormon Emigrants,
the first settlement in the Utah Territory, which included lands now called Nevada. The
Gold Rush thwarted the Mormon's westward ho, and by the time the Pony Express stop

Woodfords Fire Truck at Alpine County Museum

was established here in 1864, the place was known as Careys Mill, after John Carey who ran a lumber mill. Carey moved on when business for the Comstock Lode got slow, but left behind his name on the mountain—Careys Peak. In 1869, Daniel Woodford set up what he called the Sign of the Elephant Inn—a term making reference to mirages seen by wagon-weary emigrants. People liked the inn so much they renamed the town after him.

Woodfords, subject to canyon winds, has suffered through five devastating fires, most recently in 1989. Fire has destroyed structures, but people have remained: The Mountain Garden Bed and Breakfast is operated by Linda Merrill, whose relatives have been here since Willis P. Merrill opened a trading post in 1854.

CONTINUE WEST ON HWY. 88/89 UP WOODFORDS CANYON INTO HOPE VALLEY, PAST JCT. 88/89. CONTINUE WEST ON HWY. 88.

During emigrant years, wagons by the thousands went up Woodfords Canyon, known then as Rocky Canyon or Big Canyon. One wagoneer, having crossed the country, wrote in his diary, "This Kanyon beats all we have ever seen … We had to cut the wagon in half and use it like a cart." Halfway up Woodfords Canyon are Snowshoe Springs, named for Snowshoe Thompson who, during his 20 years crossing the Sierra alone in winter on skis, would hole up in a secret cave on the north side of the canyon.

After topping Woodfords Canyon you'll see Sorensen's Resort, first established in 1928. It is one of the oldest continuously operated resorts in the Sierra. For the last twenty years, the resort has been under the care of John and Patty Brissenden, who have done much to promote low-impact tourism and to preserve the scenic resources of the region. The resort today offers a wide-range of events and workshops, including photography, stargazing, fly-fishing, and history walks. The Norway House at Sorensen's was imported piece-by-piece from its native land.

TURN LEFT BLUE LAKES ROAD.

This begins a 16-mile loop off Hwy. 88, about 10 miles on unpaved road. If you don't want to drive unpaved road, go in 6 miles until pavement ends at Charity Valley, come out, and proceed west on Hwy. 88 to Red Lake.

Blue Lakes Road, first called Border Ruffian Pass Road, was in the Silver-boom days of the 1870s the major north-south route from the Carson Valley and Tahoe to Ebbetts Pass and Sonora. But Hope, Faith and Charity valleys were named before then. Some say the names derived from a group of Mormons returning to Utah after a tragedy at—Tragedy Springs—and who were buoyed by the beauty and ease of passage they encountered on the way down. Others say the valleys were named by a group of Masons who were racing a group of Odd Fellows to establish a charter in California in 1860. The Odd Fellows went over Carson Pass. The Masons took the route through three valleys, naming them with growing confidence on their way to Murphys Camp. Sadly, history does not record who won.

In the 1880s, Faith Valley was a dairy, where dairyman Harrison Berry is credited with the introduction to California of the square churn with baffles. Berry claimed the wild grasses of Faith and Charity valleys made for better-tasting butter than he got out of the cows back in his Midwestern home state. The method he developed for churning butter became the way it was done throughout the west.

CONTINUE TO BLUE LAKES.

At Blue Lakes in the late 1800s a race track operated during the summers near the mining towns of the day, Summit City and Harmonial City. Blue Lakes, just a few miles from Ebbetts Pass, was a crossroads for miners headed to various mining camps and way stations. Drive along the east shore of both lakes and the road will take you over Forestdale Divide and back out to the lower end of Red Lake on Hwy. 88.

AT RED LAKE, HWY. 88.

You can drive up unpaved road on south side of Red Lake or take Hwy 88 to turnout just 100 feet east of Carson Pass.

At the west end of Red Lake, just below the Carson Pass, is the scarred rocky face that symbolizes the pluck and perseverance of emigrants. Look for the marks of wagon wheels left behind on "Devils Ladder" as they hoisted their loads the last yards of a 1,000-mile journey. Donner Pass lives in infamy, but historical diaries suggest more emigrants faced Devils Ladder with trepidation.

Near here, not coincidentally, in the late 1850s John Studebaker opened a tire-setting shop with $68 capital. At this wagon-busting location, Studebaker didn't have many idle days—nor many customers who were in a position to quibble over price. He parlayed his earnings from that enterprise to establish the Studebaker Automobile Company when he returned to Indiana.

AT CARSON PASS, HWY. 88.

General John C. Fremont named this pass in honor of his scout, Kit Carson, when they passed through in 1844. From Stevens Peak—or near it—just north of the pass, Fremont and his party were the first Europeans to note the existence of Lake Tahoe. Local Washo people guided the expedition to the pass. Snowshoe Thompson monument is at the Carson Pass turnout, although the pass was seldom on his route when crossing the mountains. The Emigrant Trail followed what is now Highway 88 for about another 20 miles, until west of Silver Lake, where it diagonals northwest toward Placerville.

TURN LEFT ON WOODS LAKE ROAD, ONE-HALF MILE WEST OF CARSON PASS DRIVE TO LAKE AND COME BACK OUT TO HIGHWAY 88.

Woods lake is a cozy, forested lake, but not without its towering peaks. Lost Cabin Mine is a short walk from the picnic ground. Bring mosquito repellant in the summer.

CONTINUE WEST ON HWY 88, TO CAPLES LAKE.

James "Doc" Caples and family passed this way emigrating to California in 1849. They couldn't forget the place and came back within a couple years, building a block timber home that was visited by travelers for decades. Then two lakes—Twin Lakes—were here, separated by a narrow strip of rock. The two lakes were made one and named for Caples after the dam was put in; ironically the raised lake level submerged Doc's home site.

TURN LEFT ON KIRKWOOD ROAD, 1 MILE WEST OF CAPLES LAKE.

Kirkwood is a world-class ski resort boasting the highest base elevation and deepest average snowfall among California resorts. On the way back, check out the old Kirkwood Inn. By taking a walk around its bar you will have been in three counties: Amador, El Dorado and Alpine.

TOUR 2

WASHO COUNTRY AND ALPINE VALLEYS

Through Washo wintering grounds, Snowshoe Thompson's home site, Markleeville, and valleys reminiscent of the Alps.

Approximate time: 1.5 to 2.5 hours.

START AT DIAMOND VALLEY ROAD, ONE-HALF MILE SOUTH OF WOODFORDS ON HWY. 89/4. DRIVE PAST SCHOOL INTO DIAMOND VALLEY.

In the late 1800s, Diamond Valley, named for its shape as seen from above, was the site of six or seven homesteads and several sawmills, all servicing Virginia City, 50 miles to the north. The eastern Sierra's first irrigation ditches were constructed here by Snowshoe Thompson and Washo Indians, taking water from the West Carson at Woodfords.

Midway through the valley, where Indian Creek crosses under the road and on its south side, is Snowshoe's home site. He died here in 1876 of an undetermined illness at forty-nine. Some say it was appendicitis and others say it was pneumonia; he had been too ill to walk and had to resort to seeding his fields from horseback. He fell off and died later that day in his small cabin. Legend says that he pointed as he lay dying toward a secret silver mine near Silver Peak.

A marker commemorates the site, unless vandals have taken it again. Regardless, the important view is not of his house, but where he built it. Look in a circle. From this spot Thompson, most-accomplished among mountaineers, had access to six routes through the Sierra.

TURN RIGHT AT INDIAN CREEK ROAD, UNPAVED, AT EAST END OF DIAMOND VALLEY. CONTINUE PAST INDIAN CREEK RESERVOIR.

Among these volcanic outcroppings and piñons, the Washo wintered for centuries, trapping rabbits in droves in the sagebrush and harvesting nuts from the squat, grayish pines.

Arrowheads, made with obsidian from the Mono Lake area, and grinding rocks are common in this area. If you find Washo artifacts, or other objects from bygone pioneer days, please leave them behind.

The Washo way of life was altered forever in a few short years when the piñons were cut during wood drives to service the Comstock Lode—the river was filled with up to 150,000 cords, wood six-feet deep for four or five miles, floating north. Dutch Valley, just south of Diamond Valley, is a major community for today's Washoe Tribe of California and Nevada. The tribe has about 1,600 members today in Nevada and California, up from a low of 300 in the late 1800s. Prior to Europeans coming in 1850, the tribe's population was about 5,000, living on 1.5 million acres with Lake Tahoe as the center of their world.

STOP AT CURTZ LAKE, ON PAVED AIRPORT ROAD, ABOUT 2 MILES PAST INDIAN CREEK RESERVOIR.

At Curtz Lake are three, short self-guided nature study trails: a vegetative trail, a soil-geology trail and an aquatic trail. Signs identify the plants, which include most of those

Markleeville General Store

indigenous to the piñon pine belt. In the fall the trees are laden with pinenuts, which are found in the cones. They can be eaten right from the cone, if the birds and squirrels don't beat you to them, or oven roasted at a low temperature for a short time.

TURN LEFT ON HWY. 89/4, DRIVE TO MARKLEEVILLE. CONTINUE THROUGH TOWN.

In 1861, Jacob J. Marklee recorded 160 acres that became the town site. Other than that, his claim to fame was operating a toll ferry across the Middle Fork of the Carson River (now Markleeville Creek) and being shot dead by one H.W. Tuttle in 1864. Tuttle was acquitted after arguing self-defense.

The Alpine Hotel and Cutthroat Saloon—named for the fish, not the activity—is the original structure built in 1862 in Silver Mountain City and moved here in 1885. It's previous names were Fisk Hotel and Hot Springs Hotel. Jacob Marklee's home site is under the historic, granite blocked courthouse, built in 1928—along with the library. The Markleeville General Store which is next to the courthouse is nearly a century old, unusual since these wood-frame buildings of the Old West have often burned.

TURN RIGHT ON LARAMIE STREET.

In 1864, Silver Mountain City was voted the county seat. Markleeville had a population of about 2,600—with more than 15,000 other residents scattered in local mining districts—and some 200 homes. A telegraph line was strung to Genoa, Nevada. During the Civil War, an armory with a company of Union troops was stationed here. In 1875, when silver was demonetized, an exodus took place, dropping the area-wide population to around 1,000, a majority of whom voted to make Markleeville the county seat.

JOG RIGHT ON HOT SPRINGS ROAD, TURN LEFT, GO UP HILL

Alpine County Museum and Historical Complex is the site of Old Webster School, historic jail, and museum. The grounds are a great picnic spot and viewing area of the town. The museum holds a noteworthy collection of artifacts, photographs and documents. Just west on Hot Springs Road check out Villa Gigli for some local ambiance. Ruggero and Gina Gigli offer authentic Italian food, original artwork and genuine hospitality.

CONTINUE WEST ON HOT SPRINGS ROAD, GO 2 MILES. TURN LEFT ON PLEASANT VALLEY ROAD, CONTINUE 3 MILES INTO PLEASANT VALLEY, ABOUT 2 MILES UNPAVED.

Set below Raymond Peak and fringed with cottonwoods, conifers and large groves of aspen, Pleasant Valley combines the alpine with the bucolic. Aspen, even in the most remote of hanging vallleys throughout Alpine County, are often inscripted with the artful carvings of Basque sheepherders. The valley's display of fall color is an event worth seeing as are the trees in summer leaf when the slightest breeze starts their leaves "quaking" in the sunlight.

Creeping Aspen

Pleasant Valley was the probable route of Captain Joseph Walker on his expedition of 1833, though his records are not as detailed as those of General Fremont, who ventured through here 11 years later.

During the silver boom a few decades later, Pleasant Valley was the main route to high mining district towns, like Summit City and Silver Mountain City on Ebbetts Pass. On the south side of Pleasant Valley is Raymond Canyon, site in the late 1800s of Raymond City, large enough to have a drug store and saloon. Legend tells of a cave in this area, where Raymond City's last miners stored belongings one year—and never returned to get them. Don't count on finding it, no one else has.

GO BACK TO HOT SPRINGS ROAD. TURN LEFT, DRIVE 4 MILES TO GROVER HOT SPRINGS STATE PARK.

It is not difficult to imagine why the Washo gathered in Hot Springs Valley for generation upon generation. General Fremont encountered the amiable people there in 1844, and several Washo guided the expedition to what was then named Carson Pass. Some locals doubt this version of the story, reasoning that the meeting took place in Pleasant Valley, since the verbose Fremont did not mention hot springs in his diary.

In 1854, John Hawkins, a rancher and farmer, took up squatters' rights in Hot Springs Meadow. In 1878 the Grover family purchased the land from Hawkins, and ran a dairy. The Grovers later opened a resort in concert with the Hot Springs Hotel (which was the renamed Fisk Hotel) in Markleeville. The property twice changed hands in the 1900s— its old-growth pines and cedars were cut—and then, in 1959, was sold to California State Division of Parks and Beaches. The structure near today's pool facility dates back to around 1900.

Grover's natural mineral waters, which are cooled to just above 100 degrees before being piped into the pool, draw visitors from throughout the west, many of whom boast of the water's curative powers. Some people actually drink it, though this is not commonly recommended. The facility, which includes a cold pool alongside the hot, is open year around with the exception of Christmas, Thanksgiving and New Year's. The campground is open all year.

Harry Hawkins' Cabin

TOUR 3
HISTORIC MINING DISTRICTS

Into Mogul and Monitor Mining Districts, to Dixon Mine in Wolf Creek, Chalmers Mansion and Silver Mountain City, and Bear Valley.

Approximate time: 3 to 4 hours.

START AT MARKLEEVILLE, GO SOUTH ON HWY 89/4. TURN LEFT ON HWY. 89 TOWARD MONITOR PASS.

At the turnoff to Monitor Pass stood the town of Mt. Bullion. Across the river is evidence of a mining tunnel dating back to the 1860s. A post office was set up here in 1869, called "Bullionia," but it didn't stop the town from vanishing by 1873.

CONTINUE UP HWY 89 FOR 2 MILES. TURN LEFT TOWARD LOOPE CANYON ON FOREST SERVICE ROAD 190.

Note: This begins 8 miles off road. If you'd rather drive pavement, continue on Hwy. 89, 4 miles to the Leviathan Mine Road, which is 2 miles above Heenan Lake.

At this turnoff, where you will see evidence of recent mine workings, was the town of Monitor—later named Loope. Telegraph and Wells Fargo offices were established here in 1865. With a population of 2,500 in 1864, Monitor finished a close third in the voting to become county seat. The town was abandoned in 1888, but begun anew in 1898, when a Dr. Loope arrived representing Eastern investors. This attempt to rekindle mining was not successful, due to faltering backers and poor ore, and not helped at all by fires and floodwaters.

CONTINUE ON ROAD 090, TAKING RIGHT FORKS AS MAJOR OPTIONS ARISE. THEN TURN RIGHT ON LEVIATHAN MINE ROAD 052, AND DRIVE BACK OUT TO HWY. 89, 2 MILES ABOVE HEENAN LAKE.

Scossa Cow Camp

Climbing up from the highway through the old Mogul Mining District, you'll pass a left turn to a recently worked Cal/Silver Mine, and then Curtz Mine and Morningstar Mine. Use extreme caution at mine sites and heed private property signs.

TURN LEFT ON HWY. 89 TO MONITOR PASS.

On the south side of Monitor Pass are some roads dipping into the upper Monitor District, and also leading to the Dump Canyon route of the camel trains. Just east of the pass is the road to Leviathan Peak, and the relatively short hike to the magnificent view from the peak's lookout station. (See the introduction to the Markleeville trailheads for more information about Monitor Pass.)

TURN BACK TOWARD MARKLEEVILLE. CONTINUE TO HEENAN LAKE.

Note the poster-quality view at the historical marker in the aspens as you come west on Monitor.

Heenan Lake, which now is the only Lahontan Cutthroat brood stock lake in California, was in the late 1800s the entrance to the lower Monitor District mines in Lexington and Monitor canyons. Bagley Valley ranch, with its Vaquero Camp, predated the miners in the region.

CONTINUE DOWN TO HIGHWAY 89. TURN LEFT AT HWY. 4 TO WOLF CREEK ROAD. DRIVE IN 6 MILES, 3 MILES UNPAVED, AND FOLLOW SIGNS TO DIXON MINE.

The campground at Centerville, at the turnoff on Hwy. 4, was once the mining town of the same name. The main road to Bodie, near Bridgeport, came through here and into Wolf Creek and Silver King Valley. Dixon Mine, below the southern end of Wolf Creek Meadow, is of more recent lineage. It is set dramatically in the river canyon, with workings on both sides of the river.

DRIVE BACK TO HWY.4, TURN LEFT, GOING WEST ON HWY. 4.

Chalmers Mansion is marked by the tall brick smokestack that was once used in connection with a nearby silver ore reduction plant. Lord Chalmers, an Englishman, came to Alpine in 1867 to develop mining property on behalf of investors in London. He first worked the Mt. Bullion and Monitor districts, but in 1870 purchased mines near Silver Mountain City. By 1880 London investors had poured in thousands more dollars, allowing Chalmers and his new bride, former housekeeper Mrs. Laughton, to live well. But no rich strike materialized. In 1885 Chalmers returned to London to raise more money, but died instead. Mrs. Chalmers and the couple's child became destitute and moved to San Francisco.

Scossa Cow Camp, the picturesque ranch house and corral just up the road, is a working concern. Snowshoe Thompson's widow, Agnes, married into the Scossa family around 1880.

West of Scossa Camp, is the site of Silver Mountain City, Alpine's county seat from 1864 to 1875. Scandinavian miners first settled here in 1858, naming it Konesberg (various spellings). Snowshoe Thompson bested some of his fellow Norsemen in a ski contest here at "jump rock." This was the first known ski competition in the United States. By 1863 the Silver Mountain District town had 50 or 60 buildings, some 15,000 people, and 300 mining claims. The richest of the claims was in IXL Canyon.

CONTINUE WEST AT EBBETTS PASS ON HWY. 4.

The first European man known to cross the Sierra, Jedediah Smith, did so here in 1827. But the route was named for Major John Ebbetts who crossed in 1849 leading a group from Knickerbocker Exploring Company of New York. This route may well have become the first railroad crossing of the Sierra. In 1853, Major Ebbetts was retained by the Atlantic and Pacific Railroad Company to survey and begin. But early in 1854 Ebbetts drowned on Petaluma Creek near San Francisco when his steamer ship blew up.

West of Ebbetts Pass is the trail leading north to Border Ruffian Flat, once a hideout for the fabled Murietta Gang. This is where the road from Summit City and Blue Lakes joins with Ebbetts.

CONTINUE DOWN HIGHWAY 4 ANOTHER 14 MILES TO LAKE ALPINE AND BEAR VALLEY.

Bear Valley is a major ski resort and home to many of Alpine's best cultural events, including, Reggae on the Mountain Spring Break, High Sierra Music Festival and Bear Valley Music Festival. You can combine a swim in Lake Alpine or bike ride around the village with viewing a first-class performance of *La Boheme* held under a circus-size tent in the tall cool pines.

These recreational and cultural gatherings are in contrast to the area's history as an out-of the-way place. Bear Valley was home to the last grizzly bear spotted in California. It was also a remote way station on Big Tree Road operated by Harvey Blood, and, after that, the region was used as a getaway for Alpine's renegade recluse, Monty Wolf.

TOUR 4

BODIE, MONO LAKE AND RURAL NEVADA

To the ghost town of Bodie, tufas of Mono Lake, waterfowl havens of Bridge-port and Topaz lakes and down the east side of the Sweetwater Mountains through rural Nevada.

Approximate time: 6 or 7 hours.

START AT MARKLEEVILLE, TAKE HWY. 89 OVER MONITOR PASS TO JCT. HWY. 395. TURN RIGHT AND CONTINUE SOUTH ON HWY. 395 THROUGH COLEVILLE, WALKER AND WEST WALKER RIVER CANYON. *If Monitor is closed, take Hwy. 88 to Gardnerville and proceed south on Hwy. 395.*

West Walker River Canyon was the route of Captain Joseph Walker, whose expedition in 1833 was the first known exploration of the Sierra; his poorly documented route continued northwest through Alpine. This rugged canyon was cataclysmically altered by the flood of New Year's Day, 1998.

Bridgeport Lake

CONTINUE SOUTH ON HWY. 395 TO BRIDGEPORT.

Bridgeport is the big city for recreational tourists in the summer, with several good Ameri-can fare restaurants, as well as a well-stocked sporting goods store. A good spot to replen-ish picnic supplies or grab a frosty cone after along day of hiking. The late 1800s was Bridgeport's boom period. Known then as the logging town of Big Meadows, Bridgeport supplied Aurora and Bodie with some 50,000 cords of wood, as well as millions of board feet of lumber. Bridgeport is big views, cattle grazing ranchlands, wide open spaces.

A back road to Bodie, Aurora Canyon Road, leaves east from Bridgeport near Bridgeport Lake. Bridgeport's courthouse, still a working building, was built in 1880, after it was learned that Aurora was in Nevada and therefore could not be the county seat.

TURN LEFT 7 MI. SOUTH OF BRIDGEPORT ON BODIE ROAD, DRIVE IN 13 MILES.

Gold was discovered here in 1859 by Mr. Bodie, who died in a blizzard a few months later. The silver discovery at the Comstock Lode drew resources and attention, while a series of mining ventures failed here over the ensuing years, including one by Leland Stanford. In 1877, an accidental cave-in at Standard Mine revealed a rich quartz ledge. Another rush was on.

During the next dozen years, Bodie's heyday, some $30 million in gold and silver was mined, equaling about $700 million in today's values. Some 12,000 miners roamed the hills and town, which claimed the wildest streets and worst weather in the West. Bodie State Historical Park preserves much of the mining town virtually intact, as if people just walked away.

LEAVE BODIE SOUTH ON GRADED COTTONWOOD CANYON RD., GO 12 MILES, **TURN RIGHT** ON HWY. 167, GO EAST SEVERAL MILES AND **TURN LEFT** ON CEMETERY ROAD TO THE COUNTY PARK AT MONO LAKE.

A short walk leads to some of the tufa towers, calcium carbonate growths caused by a chemical reaction between minerals in the lake and underwater springs. Mono, which has no outlet, is mineral-rich. It was some 600-feet deeper when glacier melt filled it, and before water from major creeks was diverted to Southern California. Due to efforts of the Mono Lake Committee and other conservationists, this diversion has largely ceased and the lake level is rising. At least a million water birds visit Mono, many drawn by its population of brine shrimp.

CONTINUE WEST TO HWY. 395, TURN LEFT AND GO 3 MILES. TURN LEFT AT MONO LAKE VISITORS CENTER.

The visitors center, itself a sight to see perched above the east shore of the lake, has a very good bookstore and several natural history presentations. The back patio of the center is a spectacular viewing area. For other places to visit in the Mono Lake area, see Trailhead 57.

*Bodie
Cemetery*

GO NORTH ON HWY. 395 OVER CONWAY SUMMIT TO BRIDGEPORT. VEER RIGHT ON HWY. 182, SWEETWATER ROAD.

Bridgeport Lake is a popular fishing lake, and also a major rest stop and wintering ground for migrating waterfowl. In the old days, cordwood for the mines was floated across the lake. Departing the lake, the road takes you up the east side of the Sweetwater Mountains—on the west side is the Walker River Canyon. The Sweetwaters, underrated fly-fishing and hiking country, are visible to the southeast from many Alpine peaks and are sometimes mistaken for the White Mountains, because of their granite slopes.

CONTINUE—HWY 182 BECOMES HWY. 338 IN NEVADA—TO WELLINGTON.

Wellington is at the southern end of Smith Valley, which, along with Mason Valley in Yerington, is a farming greenbelt stuck between the Pine Nut Range and the Great Basin. The bar and restaurant in Wellington, a well-known watering hole, draws people from Reno and Carson City who are looking to revisit the hospitality of old Nevada.

TURN LEFT OR WEST ON HWY. 207 TO HWY. 395.

At Hwy. 395, you can jog left a few miles to Topaz Lake. The large lake is popular among water skiers and boat fishermen, and its southern shore marshes are a landing zone for waterfowl and other birds. Topaz Lake Lodge is a lively casino known for its view and seafood buffet.

CONTINUE NORTH ON 395 THROUGH MINDEN/GARDNERVILLE, TO JCT. HWY 88. GO SOUTH ON HWY. 88 TO RETURN TO MARKLEEVILLE.

Sharkey's Casino in Gardnerville is something of a landmark, with its western and boxing memorabilia and 20-pound prime rib dinners. The casino is also home to a fine collection of circus posters and western saddles. Oil portraits of American Indian chiefs and vintage black and white photos line the walls. Live band music can be heard every Friday and Saturday night. Along the main drag you'll also see a couple of Basque restaurants where five-course meals are served family style and picon punch is the recommended aperitif.

TOUR 5

CARSON WAY STATIONS TO THE COMSTOCK LODE

Along old way-station route, through Nevada's oldest town, railroads in Carson City, and to Virginia City, capital of the Comstock.

Approximate time: 4 to 6 hours.

START AT WOODFORDS AND GO EAST ON HWY. 88. GO 3 MILES, AND TURN LEFT AT BOTTOM OF HILL WHERE HWY. 88 REACHES CARSON VALLEY. TURN RIGHT, IMMEDIATELY. CONTINUE NORTH ON FOOTHILL ROAD TO KINGSBURY GRADE.

Ironically, the first emigrants to chronicle this route were eastbound. In 1848, several hundred Mormon soldiers who had been recruited to fight in the Mexican-American war returned from Southern California, seeking a route better than over the north side of Tahoe, which crossed the Truckee River too many times. They came through Hope Valley, then unnamed, and proceeded north along the west edge of the Carson Valley before turning east for Salt Lake.

A few years later, west-bound Mormon emigrants returned seeking to establish Brigham Young's empire in California. But travelers to the Gold Rush, and later the Comstock Lode, came into conflict with the Mormons. Remote lands became not so remote. From 1850 to 1857, the Carson Valley saw bitter disputes between Mormons and non-Mormon settlers competing for business.

As you drive Foothill Road north, keep on the lookout for historical markers. You'll see one for Thomas and Elzy Knott, millwrights from the Midwest whose far-sighted businesses were cut short by conflicts with the Mormons; Elzy Knott was shot dead while playing poker. Another marker commemorates Lucky Bill Thorrington, an associate of the Knott's who ran a way station. Thorrington was convicted of horse thievery, in a Mormon tribunal, and hung. Snowshoe Thompson worked with the Knott's and Thorrington. Aside from markers, look for old poplar trees, which are sign of former emigrant homesteads.

CONTINUE PAST KINGSBURY GRADE.

Walley's Hot Springs Resort dates from 1862, its mineral waters having warmed guests ranging from Ulysses S. Grant and Mark Twain, to Clark Gable and a number of modern entertainers who come over Kingsbury after headlining at Tahoe's casinos. A number of pools varying in temperature overlook the valley.

CONTINUE TO GENOA.

Established in 1851 and first called Mormon Station, Genoa is Nevada's oldest permanent settlement. Mormon Station Historic State Monument features a restoration of the original trading post, with a number of artifacts, including a pair of Snowshoe Thompson's oaken skis—then called snowshoes. The park and stockade, normally a quiet picnic spot, comes alive on the Fourth of July during Genoa's annual, free concert. Across the street from the park is another museum, and a walk around Genoa's back streets will reveal a number of historic buildings, including the oldest bar in Nevada.

As you leave Genoa, look for the community cemetery to visit the memorials of the valley's pioneers, including that of Snowshoe Thompson, his wife, Agnes, and son, who died at age 11. Next to Snowshoe's grave, look for a crude granite marker, roughly inscribed "Bill," which may be the grave of Lucky Bill Thorrington, whose body was secreted away by friends after his execution.

CONTINUE NORTH ON JACK'S VALLEY ROAD UNTIL THE ROAD TURNS EAST AND MEETS HWY. 395. TURN LEFT OR NORTH INTO CARSON CITY.

Across from Fairview Street you'll see the large complex for the Nevada State Railroad Museum, which features a number of engines and cars, mostly from the Virginia & Truckee Railroad, the short line that serviced the Comstock Lode. The large grounds are encircled by a track, on which visitors can take a ride during the summer.

A mile or two north of the railroad complex, just past the silver-domed state capitol building, is the Nevada State Museum, one of the finest in the West. Natural and human history are both exhibited, from prehistoric times to the late 1800s. The museum building originated as a U.S. Mint, coining the famous Carson City silver dollars. Massive steel shutters still remain as does the original press which occasionally mints commemorative coins. The museum's gold mine replica is a kid's favorite. Inside you'll also find exhibits displaying a wide range of historical artifacts, including Dat-So-La-Lee baskets, cowboy gear, gaming memorabilia and prehistoric skeletons of a mammoth and giant ichthysaurous—a dinosaur fish that swam when Nevada was under the sea. A children's museum is located across the street, a few blocks north.

Two blocks south of the museum is the State Capitol Building which houses the Governor's office and various other departments of state government. Large shade trees make the surrounding gardens a quiet respite on hot summer days. Be sure to visit the small museum on the second floor. The marble halls house portratis of every Nevada governor. Other buildings in the complex include the handsome Supreme Court Library and newly renovated State Legislature building.

CONTINUE NORTH ON CARSON STREET, TURN RIGHT ON HWY. 50, EAST.

After two blocks, past Roop Street, you'll see Mills Park on the right. Here, during the summer, children might enjoy the Carson Narrow Gauge Railroad, a steam locomotive that rides through the cottonwoods of Mills Park.

CONTINUE EAST ON HWY. 50, TURN LEFT, NORTH, ON HWY. 342 TO VIRGINIA CITY.

Gold was discovered here in 1850, but at that time only a few miners prospected, most choosing instead the richer placers of the Mother Lode in California. Among the local miners were Henry "Old Pancakes" Comstock, James "Old Virginny" Fennimore, Alan and Hosea Grosch, and Sandy Bowers, who was later to wed the notorious Eilley Orrum, the Washo seeress. Eilley ran a boarding house. Most of the miners were annoyed by a blue-black rock that confounded attempts to mine gold. Only the Grosch brothers knew this black stuff was silver, but, alas, Hosea died in an accident and Alan died crossing the Sierra to assay his riches. Snowshoe Thompson saved Alan's traveling partner, but was a few hours late to save the remaining Grosch.

General Ulysses S. Grant (third from left) in Virginia City

After the Grosch brothers died, existence of silver was revealed, and Henry Comstock, Fennimore, Bowers and a few others were sitting on a fortune. Alas, again, all sold out for peanuts to San Francisco financiers, and only Bowers, under the wing of the shrewd Eilley Orrum, realized any money.

To this day, the Comstock Lode is the richest deposit of minerals ever discovered. During the first ten years of the strike, San Francisco doubled in size to nearly 400,000 people, at a time when the population of Los Angeles was less than 5,000.

In spite of fires, Virginia City remains preserved as a lively tourist attraction, with old buildings, mining works, cemeteries, and miles of underground shafts—as well as private museums, curio shops, bars, snack stands and restaurants.

The Virginia & Truckee Railroad runs a short trip, and there are several old mansions and tours of original businesses, such as one of the Territorial Enterprise, where Mark Twain wrote as a young man under the tutelage of Dan DeQuille. Virginia City's camel races, which take place in mid-September, are symbolic of the wide-open, eclectic nature of the place. Most of the attractions are in a ten-block radius of the downtown area.

**TWO ALTERNATIVES
TO RETURN FROM VIRGINA CITY:**

1. CONTINUE NORTH ON 341, OVER GEIGER GRADE TO HWY. 395. TURN LEFT OR SOUTH ON 395, AT WASHOE VALLEY, TURN RIGHT ON FRANKTOWN ROAD TOWARD BOWERS MANSION.

A couple miles south on Franktown Road is Bowers Mansion, where Eilley Orrum, the new Mrs. Sandy Bowers, built a large home and appointed it with imports from Europe. The Bowers bankrupted themselves on the mansion, which is now a county park and museum. Eilley began a slow dissipation that left her in a mental hospital in San Francisco. The grounds presently house a swimming pool, museum and shaded picnic area.

CONTINUE SOUTH ON FRANKTOWN ROAD UNTIL YOU MEET UP WITH HWY. 395 SOUTH.

ALTERNATIVE ROUTE:

2. JUST NORTH OF VIRGINIA CITY, TURN RIGHT ON SIX MILE CANYON ROAD, HWY. 79. FOLLOW ROAD TO HWY. 50, TURN RIGHT, RETURN TO HWY 395 AT CARSON CITY.

The O'Reilly brothers, competitors of Henry Comstock, worked this canyon and happened upon one of the rich, initial silver veins. The O'Reillys also sold out for very little money and met with untimely deaths within the next few years up in Montana. As you head back through the desert to Carson City, look for Sutro Tunnel, an engineering marvel. The tunnel was bored through the base of the mountains to drain water that had infiltrated the miles of Comstock shafts.

DRIVING TOUR 6

LAKE TAHOE CIRCLE

Around the 72-mile shore of the largest alpine lake in North America.

Approximate time: 4 to 5 hours.

START AT PICKETTS JCT. HWYS. 88/89 IN HOPE VALLEY. DRIVE LUTHER PASS INTO MEYERS.

You get to pick from among three tales of how Luther Pass was named: for Ira M. Luther who operated a sawmill in Carson Valley in the early 1860s; or for Mr. Luther of Sacramento, the first to cross in a wagon in 1854; or for young Lieutenant Luther, in the command of Colonel Albert Sydney Johnson, an army engineer making improvements to the toll road in 1857 who was run out of town for being a Confederate sympathizer. Regardless, when you top Luther Pass, you enter the Tahoe Basin, into which more than 60 streams and creeks flow, but only one flows out—the Truckee River at Tahoe City.

TURN RIGHT ON HWY. 89/50 AT MEYERS.

Yanks Station here was a renowned watering hole and way station. Christmas Valley, a forested section along the Truckee River, is in the shadow of Echo Summit and gets the heaviest snowfall in the basin at lake level.

CONTINUE TO THE "Y," JCT. HWY. 89/50 AND TURN RIGHT ON HWY 50 TOWARD STATELINE.

You'll pass through some of Tahoe's urban development that was in part a result of popularity brought about by the 1960 Olympics in Squaw Valley. In recent years, however, due to a bi-state Tahoe Regional Planning Agency, beautification efforts have been made, greatly enhancing the area. The marina for the Tahoe Queen, one of the lake's two paddlewheel steamers, is on Ski Run Blvd. Heavenly Valley Ski resort is a few miles up Ski Run Blvd.; there you can ride a tram up 2,000 feet for a knock-out view. For other view spots try the top of Harvey's or Harrah's at Stateline, where gourmet buffets are served.

CONTINUE PAST KINGSBURY GRADE, HWY. 207.

Kingsbury is the road over Daggett Pass, the most direct way back to Alpine County from Stateline. Perched at the top is the north entrance to Heavenly Valley Ski Resort.

CONTINUING ON HWY. 50.

To see Nevada Beach, one of the best places to appreciate Lake Tahoe, turn toward the lake at Round Hill Shopping Center, a few miles north of Kingsbury. The beach stretches from the Edgewood Golf Course, noted for its nationally televised celebrity golf tournaments, to the south end of Marla Bay. Campers can spread their tents under tall pines, install their folding chairs in just the right spot and relax with a commanding view of the lake and the west shore peaks.

Further north on Hwy. 50, around the next few bends, is Zephyr Cove with its old lodge restaurant, good swimming beach, and the M.S. Dixie, another Tahoe paddle wheeler, which travels across to Emerald Bay. Past Zephyr Cove is Cave Rock, perhaps the best boat launch and a good picnic spot.

Just as highway 50 turns east and climbs from the there lake is a private road down to Glenbrook, open to visitors. Glenbrook has short lakeside walks with good fall color. This area was the center of the logging business in the late 1800s, when Tahoe was being used for timber and fish to feed the Comstock.

CONTINUE ON HWY. 28 TOWARD INCLINE VILLAGE, PAST HWY. 50 TURNOFF TO CARSON CITY.

A few miles beyond Spooner Lake—which is a recommended fall color walk, and a popular cross-country ski area—you'll come to the improved parking area for Chimney Beach. This beach, as well as Secret Beach and some unnamed spots, are a hike down of a few hundred feet. You'll find a number of sandy coves with large granite boulders submerged in turquoise water. The sun can be very intense at this high elevation; the strongest level of sunblock is *de rigueur*.

Near Bliss State Park

CONTINUING ON HWY. 28.

You come to Sand Harbor, located a few miles after these beaches where the highway reaches lake level. Sand Harbor is a beautiful swimming beach and home to Tahoe's summer Shakespeare festival. Between Sand Harbor and Incline Village, you have a chance to visit the Ponderosa Ranch set from TV's Bonanza. Beyond Incline Village Ski Resort is Stateline north, home to smaller, old-style casinos, including the Cal Neva, notorious as a hangout for Frank Sinatra and the Rat Pack.

CONTINUE TO TAHOE CITY ON HWY. 28.

You'll drive through Kings Beach and Tahoe Vista, with their lakeside cabins and motels, and then into Carnelian Bay, where the marina features some classic vintage inboards and sail boats. Tahoe City will be the best stop for shopping and strolling. Both its main drag and lakeshore feature art galleries, fine restaurants and hip outdoor gear shops. August is traditionally *the* month to escape the city and holiday at "The Lake."

Behind the shopping center is a state park with a pier that will take you as far as you're going to get onto the lake on foot. From the end of the dock you can view the north shore's "double sunrise"—one sun that rises over the mountains, and the other which is reflected off the lake.

TURN LEFT, SOUTH, AT HWY. 89 TOWARD HOMEWOOD.

At this junction, be sure to check out the Truckee River spillway, Tahoe's only drainage. Huge trout loiter here for tourists.

Nearby is Layton State Park, a pleasant picnic spot, and Gatekeepers Cabin museum with a notable collection of Tahoe memorabilia and Indian basketry. This zone is also excellent to explore on mountain bikes, as paved bike trails lead in both directions along the lakeshore as well as north on Hwy. 89 toward Squaw Valley along the Truckee River. Family rafting down the Truckee is also popular.

CONTINUE SOUTH ON 89 BACK TO SOUTH LAKE TAHOE.

This stretch of Hwy. 89 includes the William Kent Visitors Center and Sunnyside Restaurant, two spots to enjoy the lake in different ways. Further down, just north of Meeks Bay, is Sugar Pine Point State Park, featuring the Ehrman Mansion, an example of the opulent summer homes that were built in the early 1900s, Tahoe's golden years. Old estates dot the shoreline along this westerly coast. South of Meeks Bay, with its large campground and picturesque sailboat harbor, the road leaves the lake for several miles.

Then you come to Bliss State Park. Bliss offers some short trails at the sheer lakeshore and good picnic spots. Just beyond the entrance to Bliss, are two or three turnouts with lake views and unofficial access trails. South of here you wind down to Emerald Bay, with Vikingsholm, Eagle Falls, Fallen Leaf Lake and Tallac Historic Site, all of which are mentioned in the Tahoe Trailhead Descriptions.

Alpine's Common Plants And Animals

TREES

Higher elevation

Mountain Hemlock (droopy tops)
Whitebark Pine (dwarf at timberline)
Red Fir (north facing, grouped together)
Foxtail Pine (dwarf at highest rocky areas)

Mid and Lower Elevation

Jeffry Pine (butterscotch or vanilla smell)
Lodgepole Pine (mistakenly called Tamarack)
Piñon Pine (Great Basin, pinenuts a Washo staple)
Yellow Pine (also Ponderosa, Jeffrey's west-slope cousin)
White Fir (shade and north slope)
Sierra Juniper (slow growing, most old-growths)
Incense Cedar (wet places, first choice of pioneer loggers)
Western White Pine (also Silver Pine, narrow, six-inch cones)
Sugar Pine (huge cones, rare on east slope, crest)

Deciduous

Aspen (red, orange, yellow in fall, tree-carver's and beavers' favorite)
Alder (in wet places, bush-like)
Cottonwood (low elevation, a sign of water)

Weathered Juniper

FLOWERS

All habitats, many varieties

> Lupine
> Violets

Wet habitats

> Columbine
> Shooting Star
> Tiger Lilly
> Douglas Iris
> Corn Lily
> Rein Orchid
> Buttercup
> Monkey Flower
> Evening Primrose
> Swamp Onion
> Cow Parsnip
> Delphinium

Grover Hot Springs Meadow

Moist Habitats

> Death Camas
> Cinquefoil
> Wild Rose
> Aster
> Blue Dicks
> Larkspur
> Sierra Primrose (rocky)
> Red Heather (rocky)
> White Heather
> Ithuriel's Spears
> Snow Plant (shade)

Dry Habitats

> Pride of the Mountains
>   (high, rocky, also Pentstemon)
> Mule Ear
> Paintbrush (many varieties)
> Phlox
> Yarrow
> Mariposa Lily
> Scarlet Gilia
> Fireweed
> Flax
> Stickseed
> Prickly Poppy
> Sulfur Plant
> Green Gentian

BIRDS

Nesting in Alpine

All Season

Bald Eagle
Golden Eagle
Red-Tailed Hawk
Great Horned Owl
California Quail
Clark's Nutcracker
Stellar's Jay
Piñon Jay
American Dipper
Robin
White-headed Woodpecker
Canada Goose
Water Ouzel

Mostly Summer

Blue Grouse
Turkey Vulture
Common Merganser
American Kestrel
Spotted Sandpiper
Common Nighthawk
Calliope Hummingbird
Cliff Swallow
Barn Swallow
Mountain Bluebird
Red-winged Blackbird
Brewer's Blackbird
Western Tanager
Purple Finch

*Lists provided with help
of naturalist Paula Pennington*

CRITTERS

Mule Dear
Black Bear
Coyote
Bobcat
Mountain Lion
Marmot
California Ground Squirrel
Golden Mantle
    Ground Squirrel
Gray Squirrel (in trees)
Chipmunk
Short-tailed Weasel
Badger
Red and Grey Fox
Beaver (introduced)
Cottontail
Jackrabbit
Raccoon
Porcupine

*California
Ground
Squirrel*

Mountain Coyote

Mule Deer

Free Hiking Advice and Opinion

GEAR

Never take new boots out of the box and start hiking … Break in new boots by wearing them around the house and while driving … Get boots with Gore-Tex lining … Boots should feel good to stand in right off the bat … Unless you are a mountain climber, external frame packs are better than internal frame for backpacking: they have more compartments, can be leaned against something and leaned on, allow air circulation on your back, and you can tie things to the frame … Butane canister stoves are easier to use than liquid gas stoves … For warmth, layer clothes, starting with polyester or silk, then down and fleece, and Gore-Tex or equivalent … Use a Thermarest pad … Pack with a tent or shelter … Hiking poles are a third leg … Throw in the backpack: garbage bags, Ziplocks, athletic tape, paper clip … A collapsible water bottle gives you flexibility in selecting camp site … Sunscreen, sunglasses, hat … Always bring food, water, and extra clothes when day hiking … Light gloves are a good idea in summer … Test stove and put up tent before leaving home … Buy a larger stuff sack than the one the tent comes in … Use synthetic sleeping bag … Carry Swiss Army knife and a flashlight … Socks: blend of acrylic, wool, stretch nylon … Golden Rule of backpacking: Take everything you need and not one thing more …

CAMP TIPS

All the usuals about not spoiling or camping near water sources … Hang stuff to dry on limbs … To break a limb for firewood, drop a big rock rather than use Kung Fu move … Camping too close to water invites mosquitoes and dew … Use wet sand to wash dishes … Never leave a rock fire ring that you built … Wilderness is about enjoyment, not roughing it … Don't camp downwind from a dead tree … Never sleep in a tent with someone who had black beans for dinner … Take off sweaty clothes and put on dry first thing in camp … Other uses for hiking poles: camp billiards, fencing, weenie roasts … Only the finest resort hotel rivals the finest campsite …

MISHAPS AND HOW TO AVOID THEM

A dog is a bear's worst friend ... Never be the tallest thing around when lightning is around ... If you see lightning in the distance, get down from the ridge ... If you can smell a forest fire you are in its path :... Carry DEET mosquito repellant and don't forget to put it on clothes ... Drinking hot liquid will warm you quicker than a fire ... The only cure for altitude sickness is lower altitude ... Ibuprofen ... Cross rivers at widest spots, not in white water or smooth fast water ... Use a stick or pole to cross river ... Don't cross water deeper than your crotch ... On loose rock slopes, groups stay close together and not directly down-slope from each other ... Stretch before, during and after hikes ... When cold, eat food ... Hiking poles save knees and ankles ... Tell someone where you're going ... Unstrap your pack when crossing a creek ... Most hypothermia happens in summer ... Fight back against a mountain lion ... Bears are dangerous if you see cubs ... You can't outrun a bear, but you might outrun the other guy ... In lightning, avoid water, high ground, metal gear and tallest trees ... Snowshoe Thompson's hypothermia prevention technique: dance on a big rock all night ... It's easier to prevent blisters and dehydration than to cure ... When cold, the first thing to cover is your head ...

TRAIL TIPS

In hot weather, dip your hat or bandana in a stream and put on head ... At noon, the sun is due south ... The top of the shadow of a vertical stick, over time, traces a line from west to east ... Moss grows on all sides of trees ... Get oriented the moment you get lost, retrace footsteps ... Mark your path off-trail as you go with little piles of rocks ... When lost, relax, don't panic, drink water ... Watch your watch to gauge your distance; know when half your time is used up ... Start early ... Sun intensity increases 5% for every 1,000 feet elevation ... You need a topographical map to walk long distances cross country ... Don't cross trail junctures until entire group has gathered ... Never cross manzanita ... Zen of hiking: A trail is the most direct path of least resistance ... Shortcuts can take twice as long; know the terrain and where you're going before heading off-trail ...

CROSS COUNTRY SKIING

Use track skis with Teflon lubricant … Layer clothes and avoid sweating … Just because you're not sweating doesn't mean you don't need water … Bring nuts, dried fruit, chocolate … Extra power bars … Extra dry socks … Know how to build a snow cave… Don't ski below a snow laden cornice … Or on top of one … Check your pockets for missing objects after you've taken a face plant . . . Wear sunscreen … Wrap duct tape around your ski pole to be used for repairs … Use caution crossing snow bridges …

FOOD AND DRINK

Eat before you're hungry … Always filter or boil drinking water … Drink before you're thirsty … Drink a lot of water … Hiking food is any without water in it … Drink a lot of water … You can buy most backpacking food in a supermarket … Eat several snacks during day, not one big lunch … The Complete John Muir Camp Cookbook: stale bread and stream water … Throw in extra trail mix or jerky … Bring iodine to treat water if pump breaks … Drink a lot of water … Never put a banana or pear in a knapsack … Indulgence is okay if you're willing to carry the load …

FEET

Your feet are your car … Cut your toenails before a hike … Soaking feet, or any appendage, in cold water will cure soreness and sprains … Bring Band Aids, moleskin, athletic tape, Neosporin … If shoes give you a blister twice, don't take them on your next hike … Take care of blister before it's a blister … Wash your socks everyday … It's hard to cross a river in bare feet; bring Tevas … Soak tired feet at lunch … Squeeze Vitamin E capsules on blisters or burns … Warming wet shoes next to the fire is a recipe for burnt sole … Don't sleep with socks on you've hiked in, they'll make your feet colder … Tao of mountain climbing: Virtue is a person with two feet who gets to the top of the hill …

WALKING

Never walk downhill with your hands in your pockets … Slow and steady wins the race … The shortest distance between two points is around … Fall up the mountain by leaning uphill, pushing off back foot, falling forward … Coming downhill, fall on your butt, not your face … Avoid walking in the heat of the day … Place feet on flat spots … If you don't know where you are, stay on trail … Stay on trail anyway … Groups never lose sight of each other, especially the slowest and fastest persons … Following deer will lead you to brush … North facing slopes lead to snow … Carry no more than one-third body weight … Never rest so long that you are tired when you start again … Tightening your stomach when you walk makes you light on your feet.

DISCLAIMER

By following the directions and engaging in the activities suggested in this book you may be bitten, burned, buoyed, bummed-out, broken, buffed, bent, befriended, bewildered, enlightened, injured, elated, energized, unnerved, lost, discovered, loved, lonely, betwixt and between. The authors and publisher can take neither credit nor blame for any of it, but sincerely do wish you the happiest of trails.

RESOURCE LINKS

ALPINE COUNTY CAMPGROUNDS

(FS) = FOREST SERVICE, (BLM) = BUREAU OF LAND MANAGEMENT

**GROVER HOT SPRINGS IS OPEN ALL YEAR.
LOWER-ELEVATION CAMPGROUNDS ARE OPEN APRIL
OR MAY THROUGH OCTOBER; HIGHER-ELEVATION (ABOVE 7000')
OPEN JUNE THROUGH SEPTEMBER.**

With piped water and flush toilets and showers

Grover Hot Springs (State), 76 sites, 5900'
    (4 mi. west of Markleeville on Hot Springs Road)
Hope Valley Resort (FS/priv), 24 sites, 6900'
    (1 mi. east of Picketts Jct. on Hwy. 88/89)
Indian Creek Reservoir (BLM), 29 sites, 5600'
    (4 mi. in Airport Rd., between Markleeville/Woodfords)

With piped water and flush toilets

Highland Lakes (FS), 35 sites, 8600'
    (7 mi. in on Highland Lakes Road, west of Ebbetts Pass)
Lake Alpine (FS), 27 sites, 5 walk-in sites, 7300'
    (near Lake Alpine Lodge, Hwy. 4, west of Ebbetts Pass)
Pine Martin-Silver Valley (FS), 58 sites, 7400'
    (at east end Lake Alpine, Hwy. 4)
Silver Tip (FS), 25 sites, 7500'
    (.75-mi. west of Lake Alpine, Hwy. 4)
Turtle Rock Park (county), 28 sites, 6100'
    (.5-mi. Turtle Rock Rd., between Markleeville/Woodfords)

With piped water and vault toilets

Bloomfield (FS), 12 sites, 7900'
(2 mi. on Highland Lakes Road, west of Ebbetts Pass)
Lower Blue Lake (PG&E), 16 sites, 8000'
Upper Blue Lake (PG&E), 32 sites, 8200'
Upper Blue Lake Dam (PG&E), 25 sites, 8200'
(10 mi. in on Blue Lakes Road, off Hwy. 88)
Caples Lake (FS), 35 sites, 7800'
(west end of Caples Lake on Hwy. 88)
Crystal Springs (FS), 20 sites, 5800'
(2 mi. west of Woodfords on Hwy. 88/89)
Hope Valley Campground (FS), 20 sites, 7200'
(3 mi. in on Blue Lakes Road, off Hwy. 88)
Kit Carson (FS), 12 sites, 6600'
(1 mi. east of Picketts Jct. on Hwy. 88/89)
Markleeville Creek (FS), 10 sites, 5500'
(1 mi. south Markleeville on Hwy, 89/4)
Middle Creek (PG&E), 6 sites, 8200'
(10 mi. in on Blue Lakes Road, off Hwy. 88)
Silver Creek (FS), 22 sites, 6800'
(on Hwy. 4, 7 mi. west jct. Hwy. 4/89)
Snowshoe Springs (FS), 13 sites, 6100'
(2 mi. east of Picketts Jct. on Hwy. 88/89)
Woods Lake (FS), 25 sites, 8200'
(2 mi. on Woods Lake Rd., 1 mi., west Carson Pass)

Stream water and vault toilets or no facilities

Centerville Flat (FS), 12 sites, 5900'
(on Hwy. 4 at Wolf Creek Road turnoff)
Hermit Valley (FS), 6 sites, 7500'
(on Hwy. 4 west of Ebbetts Pass)
Mosquito Lake (FS), 9 sites, 8200'
(on Hwy. 4, east of Lake Alpine)
Pacific Valley (FS), 6 sites, 7600'
(on Hwy. 4 east of Ebbetts Pass)

For Car Camping, Fishing, Wilderness Permits information:

Alpine County Chamber of Commerce and Visitor's Authority, 530-694-2475
3 Webster St./P.O. Box 265
Markleeville, Ca 96120
fax: 530-694-2478, www.alpinecounty.com

Open daily April through October; closed Tuesday and Wednesday during the winter.
Satellite office: Bear Valley Commercial Center, Bear Valley, California.

Grover Hot Springs State Park, 530-694-2248, 1-800-444-PARK
Turtle Rock Park Information, 530-694-2140

Forest Service/National Forest—Local Offices

Markleeville, 530-694-2475, 692-2911
Arnold, 209-795-1381
Topaz, 530-495-2447
Carson City District Office, 702-882-2766
Stanislaus National Forest/ Sonora, 209-532-3671
Toiyabe National Forest/Bridgeport, 760-932-7070
Inyo National Forest/Lee Vining, 760-647-6525, 647-3044
El Dorado National Forest, 530-644-6048
Tahoe Basin Management Unit, 530-573-2600

Yosemite National Park Wilderness Center, 209-372- 0200

Inyo Wilderness Permits, 1-888-374-3773

PG&E Campgrounds, 916-446-6616

Statewide Offices

National Parks, 818-597-9192, ext. 201
State Parks, 916-653-6995
Forest Service, 415-705-2874 or 2869
Forest Service Campgrounds, 1-800-280-CAMP
Bureau of Land Management, 916-979-2800, 702-885-6000
Department of Fish and Game, 916-355-0978, 760-872-1171

CONSERVATION GROUPS

Alpine Scenic Alliance
    Box 485
    Markleeville, CA 96120

Friends of Hope Valley
    Box 431
    Markleeville, CA 96120

Sierra Nevada Alliance, 530-694-4546
    Box 7989
    South Lake Tahoe, CA 96158

Mono Lake Committee ˙
    Box 29
    Lee Vining, CA 83541

League to Save Lake Tahoe, 530-577-1061
    989 Tahoe Keys Blvd., Suite 6
    South Lake Tahoe, CA 96150

Sierra Club, 510-848-0800 (Berkeley)
    Box 52968
    Boulder, CO 80322-2968

Wildlife Care, 530-577-2273
    Box 10577
    South Lake Tahoe, CA 96158

OUTFITTERS/GUIDES/ACTIVITIES

FISHING GUIDES & SCHOOLS

Horse Feathers, 530-694-2399
    Judy Warren
    20505 Hwy. 89
    Markleeville, CA 96120

Alpine Cowgirl

Alpine Fly Fishing, 530-542-0759
    1219 Tata Lane/Box 10465
    South Lake Tahoe, CA 96150

Alpenglow Angling, 209-474-0608

Fly Fishing Workshops at Sorensen's Resort
    1-800-423-9949, 530-694-2203

FISHING LICENSES

Sorensen's Resort, 1-800-423-9949, 530-694-2203
Woodfords Station, 530-694-2930
Markleeville General Store, 530-694-2448
Grover's Corner, 530-694-2562
East Fork Resort, 530-694-2229
Caples Lake Resort, 209-258-8888
Lake Alpine Lodge, 209-753-6237
Bear Valley Sports Shop, 209-753-2844
Bear Valley Adventure Co., 209-753-2834

RAFTING

Ahwahnee Whitewater (rafting), 209-533-1401
    (at East Fork Resort in summer)
    Box 1161
    Columbia, CA 95310

Sunshine Rafting Adventures, 1-800-829-7238, 209-848-4800
    Box 1445
    Oakdale, CA 95361

River Adventures & More (RAM), 1-800-466-7238
    Box 5283
    Reno, NV 89513

Also call Carson and Bridgeport Ranger Districts for rafting companies.

SKIING, BIKING, CLIMBING & KAYAKS

Hope Valley Outdoor Center, 530-694-2266
        (cross-country, mountain bikes, kayaks)
        14655 Hwy. 88
        Hope Valley, CA 96120

Kirkwood Resort, 209-258-6000

Kirkwood Cross Country Skiing, 209-258-7248

Alta Alpina Cycling Club
        (Death Ride co-sponsor)
        Box 2032
        Minden, NV 89423

Bear Valley Adventure Co., 1-209-753-2834
        (cross country, mountain bikes, kayaks)
        Hwy. 4 and Bear Valley Rd./Box 5120
        Bear Valley, CA 95223

Bear Valley Ski Company, 209-753-2301
        (downhill resort)
        Box 5038
        Bear Valley, CA 95223

Mountain Adventure Seminars, 209-753-6556, 1-800-36-CLIMB
        (climbing, backcountry skiing and packing)
        Box 5102
        Bear Valley, CA 95223

HORSE STABLES & GUIDES

Little Antelope Pack Station, 530-495-2443, 702-782-8977
        Box 179   .
        Coleville, CA 96107

Kirkwood Stables, 209-258-6000

Adventures on Your Horse, 1-888-554-2972

Leavitt Meadows Pack Station, 530-495-2257

Virginia Lakes Pack Station, 760-937-0326, 702-867-2591

WILDFLOWER HIKES

Sorensen's Resort, 1-800-423-9949

Grover Hot Springs, 530-694-2248

CAR SHUTTLE SERVICE - The Consortium, 530-694-2966

MUSEUM AND HISTORIC ACTIVITIES

Alpine County Museum and Historical Complex, 530-694-2102
Box 24, Markleeville, CA 96120

Emigrant Trail History Tours, 1-800-423-9949, 530-694-2203

John Muir & Mark Twain Speak, 1-800-423-9949, 530-694-2203

Bodie State Historic Park, 760-647-6445

Bower's Mansion County Park, 702-849-1825

Mono County Museum, 760-932-5281

Mono Lake Visitors Center, 760-647-3044

Mormon Station Historic Park, 702-782-2590

Museum and Historic Activities, cont'd

Tahoe-Douglas Chamber of Commerce, 702-588-4591

Lake Tahoe Visitors Authority, 1-800- AT-TAHOE

Virginia City Chamber of Commerce, 702-847-0311

ACCOMMODATIONS

Hope Valley and Woodfords

Sorensen's Resort, 1800-423-9949, 530-694-2203
    14255 Hwy. 88
    Hope Valley, CA 96120

Hope Valley Resort, 1-800-423-9949, 530-694-2203
    14655 Hwy. 88
    Hope Valley, CA 96120

Diamond Valley House, 1-800-423-9949
    c/o Sorensen's Resort
    14255 Hwy. 88
    Hope Valley, CA 96120

Mountain and Garden Bed & Breakfast, 530-694-0012
    250 Old Pony Express Rd.
    Woodfords, CA 96120

Woodfords Inn, 530-694-2410
    20960 Hwy. 89
    Markleeville, CA 96120

Kirkwood and Silver Lake

Kirkwood Resort, 209-258-6000
    1501 Kirkwood Dr./Box 1
    Kirkwood, CA 95646

Kirkwood Accommodations, 209-258-8575
　　1430 Kirkwood Dr., Box 36
　　Kirkwood, CA 95646

Kit Carson Lodge, 209-258-8500, 530-676-1370 (winter)
　　Hwy. 88 at Silver Lake
　　Kit Carson, CA 95644

Plasses Resort, 209-258-8814
　　30001 Plasses Rd., Box 261
　　Silver Lake, CA 95666

Markleeville

Alpine Inn, 530-694-2150
　　14820 Hwy. 89/Box 367
　　Markleeville, CA 96120

East Fork Resort, 530-694-2229
　　12399 Hwy. 89/Box 457
　　Markleeville, CA 96120

Grandma's House, 530-694-2253
　　14800 Hwy. 89/Box 307
　　Markleeville, Ca 96120

J Marklee Toll Station, 530-694-2507
　　Downtown Markleeville/Box 395
　　Markleeville, CA 96120

Bear Valley

Bear Valley Lodge, 209-753-2325
    3 Bear Valley Rd./Box 5440
    Bear Valley, CA 95223

Lake Alpine Lodge, 209-753-6358
    4000 Hwy. 4/Box 5300
    Bear Valley, CA 95223

Red Dog Lodge, 209-753-2344
    148 Bear Valley Rd./Box 5034
    Bear Valley, CA 95223

RESTAURANTS, CAFES, SALOONS

Sorensen's Country Café, 1-800-423-9949, 530-694-2203

Sierra Pines, 530-694-2949
    19750 Hwy. 89
    Markleeville, CA 96120

Alpine Hotel/Cutthroat Saloon, 530-694-2150
    Montgomery St. & Hwy. 89/Box 261
    Markleeville, CA 96120

The Deli, 530-694-2505
    14811 Hwy. 89/Box 18
    Markleeville, CA 96120

Alpine Restaurant, 530-694-2150
    Box 272
    Markleeville, CA 96120

Caples Lake Resort, 209-258-8888

Kirkwood Inn, 209-258-7304

Restaurants, Cafes, Saloons, cont'd

Villa Gigli, 530-694-2253
    145 Hot Springs Rd./Box 307
    Markleeville, CA 96120

Woodfords Station, 530-694-2930
    Pony Express Road
    Woodfords, CA 96120

Lake Alpine Lodge, see Accommodations
Red Dog Lodge, see Accommodations

STORES

Hope Valley Resort, see Accommodations

Rudden's Markleeville General Store, 530-694-2448
    14799 Hwy. 89/Box 547
    Markleeville, CA 96120

Grover's Corner, 530-694-2562
    14841 Hwy. 89/Box 89
    Markleeville, CA 96120

Sierra Pines, see Restaurants
East Fork Resort, see Accommodations
Woodfords Station, see Restaurants

Bear Valley General Store, 209-753-2842
    1 Bear Valley Rd./Box 5242
    Bear Valley, CA 95223

Bear Valley Sports Shop, 209-753-2844
    Box 5096
    Bear Valley, CA 95223

MAPS, CARDS, BOOKS, GIFTS

Sorensen's Resort, see Accommodations

U.S. Geological Survey Topographical Maps, 1-800-USA-MAPS or 1-888-ASK-USGS

Wilderness Press (Maps and Guidebooks), 1-800-443-7227
mail@wildernesspress.com

Carson Ranger District (Maps), 702-882-2766

Bridgeport Ranger District (Maps), 619-932-7070

Rudden's Markleeville General Store, see Stores

The Consortium, 530-694-2966
(also car-shuttles)
290 C Old Pony Express Road
Markleeville, CA 96120

The Bear's Den, 209-753-2346
3 Bear Valley Rd./Box 5253
Bear Valley, CA 95223

LOCAL CONTACTS

Friends of the Library, 530-694-2120
Box 187
Markleevillee, CA 96120

Alpine County Arts Commission, 530-694-2787
3 Webster Street/Box 546
Markleeville, CA 96120

Alpine Enterprise, 530-694-0545
(monthly newspaper)

Markleeville Post Office, 530-694-2125
Road Conditions, 1-800-427-7623
CalTrans at Woodfords, 1-530-694-2241
Alpine County Sheriff's Office, 530-694-2231
Alpine County Clerk, 530-694-2281
Alpine County Health Department, 530-694-2146
Markleeville Fire Station, 530-694-2223
Woodfords Fire Station, 530-694-2922
Bear Valley Fire Station, 209-753-2232
Kirkwood Fire Station, 209-258-8534
Alpine Unified School District, 530-694-2238
Alpine Children's Center, 530-694-2390
Great Basin Internet Services, 1-888-477-7299

MARKLEEVILLE DEATH RIDE

One summer morning in 1974, Woodfords cyclist Wayne Martin got on his ten-speed and led a few out-of-town friends on a little ride. That evening—after pedaling for 129 miles and climbing more than 16,000 feet—one of Martin's friends protested, "That was a death ride!"

Today it is *The* Death Ride, one of California's premier cycling events. Since those cult beginnings, some 50,000 cyclists have made the grueling ride, gutting it up and down five mountain passes in one day.

In the early days, The Death Ride was a race, with a predawn shotgun blast heralding a simultaneous start for all riders. But in 1986, with more than 1,000 cyclists in an all-out contest for the best time, the California Highway Patrol determined that the ride might literally live up to its name if things weren't toned down a bit. Since then, the race has been changed to a tour, with staggered starts and options to ride fewer than five passes.

The Death Ride is limited to 2,500 avid riders. Currently, the course covers Monitor Pass, over and back, and then up and down Ebbetts, Carson and Luther passes. A barbecue celebration is held at Turtle Rock Park after the tour, which lasts at least until the last bent-over cyclist makes it back. Counting families and friends who join the contestants, the county population more than quadruples on the July weekend.

EVENTS

Contact Alpine County Chamber of Commerce, 530-694-2475, or call event sponsor.

New Year's Eve ~ Torchlight Parade, Kirkwood
March ~ Snowshoe Thompson Family Ski (Hope Valley Ski Center)
Spring Break ~ Reggae on the Mountain, Bear Valley
Spring Break ~ Kirkwood Jamming Party
Memorial Day ~ Masters Road Race, Bear Valley
Late March ~ Extreme Ski Competition, Kirkwood
Summer ~ Friends of Hope Valley Music Festival, Sorensen's
July Fourth ~ High Sierra Music Festival, Bear Valley
Second weekend of July ~ Markleeville Death Ride, *www.deathride.com*
Late July through August ~ Bear Valley Music Festival
Late August ~ Bear Valley Fat Tire Fest
Labor Day weekend ~ Bear Valley Triathlon
Mid-September ~ Kirkwood Rodeo
Late September ~ Octoberfest, Bear Valley
Late September ~ Woodfords Community Fair
Halloween ~ Markleeville Childrens' Parade
Fall ~ NASA Stargazing and Watercolor Workshops, Sorensen's
Thanksgiving ~ Sorensen's Thanksgiving Feast
Winter ~ Sled Dog Races, Hope Valley

Cabin at Sorensen's Resort

Alpine Fact Sheet

Temperatures

Highs: record 98°, summer average 85°, winter average 44°
Lows: record -22°, summer average 53°, winter average 23°

Precipitation

Average annual rainfall, 21 inches
Average annual snowfall, 7.5 feet
Average snowfall, Kirkwood, 30 feet
Record snowfall, Tamarack Lake, 73.5 feet

Elevations

Markleeville, 5,500 feet
Grover Hot Springs, 6,000 feet
Woodfords, 5,700 feet
Hope Valley, 7,000 feet
Kirkwood, 7,800 feet
Bear Valley, 7,100 feet
Highest, Sonora Peak, 11,462 feet
Lowest, Fredericksburg, 4,800 feet

Acreage

*Alpine County is nearly a half-million acres,
and 93 percent of it is public land. The sizes of the
Wilderness Areas which are partly in, or close to, Alpine County are:*

Carson Iceberg 158,628 acres
Emigrant 112,277 acres
Desolation 63,745 acres
Mokelumne 38,921 acres
Hoover 48,601 acres
Ansel Adams 15,933 acres

Glossary to Understanding Alpine Culture & Customs

WAVING: When passing another car, raise two fingers off steering wheel; applies especially when passing deputy.

FASHION FOOTWEAR: Winter, Sorels; summer, none.

NON-LIBRARY INFORMATION CENTERS: Cutthroat Saloon, Sorensen's Resort, Woodfords Station (mornings only), Post Office

SIGN OF SPRING: Turns from too damn cold to too damn hot

SIGN OF SUMMER: Snow shovels are off the porches

SOUND OF FALL: Wood splitter

SIGN OF WINTER: Cat sleeps with dog

PEAK COMMUTE TRAFFIC: Tahoe to Kirkwood, 9 a.m., Kirkwood to Tahoe 5 p.m., winter only.

CRITICAL MASS: Line forms at Grover Hot Springs.

PROPER ATTIRE: Never wear a suit in Markleeville, attorneys exempted.

HUMAN MIGRATION PATTERN: Memorial Day, incoming; Labor Day, out-going.

CAPITAL OFFENSE: Littering

VIOLENT CRIME: Dumpster diving bears

PEDESTRIAN WARNING: Look both ways before sleeping in the street.

STAR-STUDDED EVENT: Meteor shower

HAPPY JACK'S CAMPSIDE COOKBOOK

Breakfast & Snacks

COWBOY COFFEE

2 tablespoons ground coffee (drip or regular grind) per cup
plus two tablespoons extra for the pot

Add coffee to boiling water for thirty seconds.

Remove and let stand for 5 minutes. Keep near campfire so it stays hot.

Strain through sock or filter, if you have one, or add an eggshell or splash of cold water to settle the grounds.

SUNRISE SCONES

2 cups rolled oats
2 cups flour
5 tablespoons sugar
1 teaspoon cinnamon
1/2 teaspoon salt
1/2 cup oil
1/2 cup dry milk mixed with 1 cup water
1/2 cup of combination of your choice of raisins, walnuts, sunflower seeds, dried cranberries

Mix dry ingredients at home.
At campsite:
Mix milk with everything but the oil. Add oil. Grease 10 or 12 inch frying pan and pat in the mix. Score into eight sectors. Cover, bake with reflectors or cook on low heat for 20 minutes, check after 10 minutes. If bottom gets too brown adjust heat.
Serves 4 to 6.

BACON ON A STICK

1 stick, green and sharpened at one end
1 toothpick
2 strips of lean slab bacon

Poke ends of bacon strips
over sharp end of stick.
Wrap like a barber pole,
secure with toothpick.
Cook over fire to suit.
Serves 1.

GOLDEN OATMEAL

4 cups water
2 cups rolled oats, pinch salt
1 cup dried milk
1/2 golden raisins
1/2 cup banana chips
4 to 6 tablespoons brown sugar or honey

Mix oats, dried milk, salt at home.
Bring water to boil, stir in oat mix.
Add raisins and banana chips and cook
low for 5 minutes.
Remove from heat and top with
brown sugar or honey. Serves 4.

GIDDYUP PANCAKES

2 cups wheat flour, 2 cups white flour
1 cup soy flour
1 cup wheat germ
1 cup dried milk
1 egg (optional)
2 teaspoons baking powder
1 teaspoon salt
1 cup oil, 4 cups water

Mix dry ingredients at home.
Stir in water and 3/4 cup oil.
Cook on medium heat in oiled
frying pan. Serves 4 to 6.

POWER BALLS

1 cup honey
1 cup peanut butter
1 cup wheat germ
1/2 cup oat bran
2 tablespoons powdered lecithin
1/2 cup soy milk
1/2 cup carob or cocoa powder
1/2 cup sunflower seeds

Mix, roll into golfball sized nuggets and chill.
Store in airtight container on the trail.

REAL SNOW CONES

1 cup snow
(scoop a few inches under surface)
1 can frozen concentrate juice—
apple, orange or lemon
or
1 package powdered lemonade,
Koolaid or Gatorade

Fill cup with clean snow.
Sprinkle with concentrate or powder.
Eat with spoon and drink.

TURKEY JERKY TERIYAKI

3 to 4 pound turkey breast
3 tablespoons coarse salt
bottled teriyaki sauce, grated fresh ginger

Place boned breast in pan.
Salt and sauce liberally.
Sprinkle in ginger.
Let stand for 6 to 8 hours in
refrigerator. Slice meat lengthwise,
1/4-inch thick, place on cookie sheet.
Dry at 150 to 200° for 10 to 12 hours
until no moisture is left. Check
frequently. Store in airtight bag or
container in refrigerator or freezer.

SPICED TRAIL MIX

1 cup pumpkin seeds
1 cup sunflower seeds
1/4 cup sesame seeds
1/2 cup pinenuts
1 cup salted pretzel sticks, broken up
1 tablespoon sesame oil
1 tablespoon teriyaki sauce
1/2 teaspoon cayenne
garlic salt to taste

Mix all ingredients except pretzel sticks.
Bake on shallow pan for
15 minutes at 300 degrees.
Cool and add pretzel sticks
Store in airtight container.

Soups & Salads

CLAM AND BACON CHOWDER

4 cups water
4 chicken bouillon cubes
2 tablespoons dehydrated onion
2 tablespoons dried parsley
3 tablespoons cooking oil or butter
1 cup dry milk, mixed with 4 cups water
1 cup instant mashed potatoes
2 6.5-oz. cans of clams, minced
4 tablespoons bacon bits
salt and pepper
cayenne pepper

Boil 4 cups water, add bouillon cubes.
Add oil and milk, stir in potatoes,
onion, parsley, bacon.
Reduce heat and simmer
for about ten minutes.
Add clams and juice and gently heat.
Add salt, pepper, cayenne to taste.
Serves 2 or 3.

GREEK LENTIL SOUP

8 oz. lentils
2 tablespoons dried onions
2 cloves garlic, minced
1 cup sun dried tomatoes, rehydrate 20
minutes before preparation, do not drain.
5 cups water
5 vegetable bouillon cubes
1 teaspoon dried parsley
4 teaspoons dried mint leaves
1 bay leaf
2 tablespoons olive oil
1 tablespoon vinegar

Bring water to boil.
Add lentils, onion, garlic, tomatoes and
bouillon. Simmer for 20 to 30 minutes.
Add parsley, mint, bay leaf and oil and
simmer until lentils tender.
Add vinegar, remove from heat.
Let stand 5 minutes.
Serves 4.

FRENCH PEA SOUP

1 cup dried split peas
4 cups of water
1 bay leaf
2 chicken bouillon cubes
2 tablespoons dried onion
2 carrots, chopped
1 or 2 cloves garlic
1/2 teaspoon thyme
1 cup packaged herb croutons

Rinse peas and soak in 4 cups water for
several hours or overnight. Do not drain.
Add ingredients and bring to boil and
simmer for 30 minutes, until peas are soft.
Stir often when cooking.
Garnish with croutons when serving.
Serves 2.

CUCUMBER FETA SALAD

2 cucumbers
3 oz. feta cheese
2 tablespoons olive oil
8 diced Greek olives
1 tablespoon lemon juice
1 tablespoon crushed mint leaves
salt and pepper

Slice cucumbers into bowl and add
ingredients. Let marinate for one hour.
Serves 2 or 3.

PETTIGREW SALAD

2 cup dried apples
(rehydrated for 15 to 20 minutes)
2 stalks celery, chopped
1/2 cup chopped walnuts
2 tablespoons canola oil
2 tablespoons cider vinegar
salt and pepper

Add all ingredients to rehydrated apples.
Serves 3.

CARROT AND RAISIN SALAD

5 carrots, finely chopped or shredded
1/2 cup raisins
2 teaspoons dried onion
1/2 teaspoon dill weed
1/2 teaspoon sugar
3 tablespoons olive oil
3 tablespoons rice vinegar
salt and pepper

Add all ingredients in bowl and mix.
Allow salad to marinate and absorb
vinegar and herbs for about a
half-hour before serving.
Serves 3.

Main Courses

SEAFOOD GARLIC PASTA

6 to 8 cloves garlic, minced
2 tablespoons dried onion
3 tablespoons oil
2 6.5-oz. can crab
1 10-oz. can whole clams
1/2 cup dry milk mixed with 1 cup water
2 tablespoons dried parsley
1/2 stick butter (optional)
1/4 cup dry sherry
Parmesan cheese
16 oz. pasta

Get pasta water boiling in large pot.
It will take about as long as sauce.
Sauté garlic with oil.
Add milk, sherry, juice from clams,
parsley, onion, butter.
Bring to boil, simmer for 5 to 7 minutes.
Add seafood and warm.
Spoon over pasta on plates.
Add cheese.
Serves 3 to 4.

SHRIMP CREOLE

1 cup sun dried tomatoes (rehydrate)
1/2 cup dried green pepper flakes
2 cups quick rice
4 1/2 cups water
1 package cream of mushroom soup
2 or 3 4.5-oz. cans of shrimp
salt and pepper

Bring water to boil, add tomatoes, pepper
flakes and rice. Simmer for 6 minutes
Add soup mix and undrained shrimp.
Mix and heat thoroughly.
Serves 4.

VIC'S SAUSAGE & DUMPLINGS

4 cups water
16 oz. or more smoked beef sausage
4 tablespoons dried onion
1 package brown gravy mix
1 package mushroom soup mix
4 oz. dehydrated mushrooms
(cover with water to rehydrate)
3 medium carrots, sliced
3 stalks celery, sliced
(can substitute dehydrated vegetables)
Bisquick—enough for 8 to 10 biscuits

Boil water, add all ingredients except biscuit mix and sausage.
Reduce heat, simmer for 10 minutes.
Mix biscuits, drop by spoonfuls into stew, and add cut-up sausage. Simmer for 20 minutes, stirring gently. Serves 4.

SLOPPY JOES

1 lb. ground beef, frozen
3 tablespoons dehydrated onions
2 cloves garlic, minced
1 6-oz can tomato paste
1 teaspoon dry mustard
1 beef bouillon cube diluted
1 package dried Sloppy Joe mix
water according to package
salt and pepper
2 teaspoons Worcestershire sauce

Let beef thaw in pack on first day.
Brown meat and onion.
Drain off fat. Add remaining ingredients. Cover and simmer for about one-half hour until thick. Stir occasionally to keep from sticking.
Serve on buns or over rice.
Serves 4.

CHICKEN CURRY

1 cup instant rice
1/2 cup raisins
1/4 cup dried apricots
1/4 cup dried apples
1/4 cup salted peanuts
4 tablespoons oil
4 cups water
2 packages chicken noodle soup
2 tablespoons curry
2 10-oz. cans boned chicken

Sauté rice and fruits in oil.
Add water, soup mixes, curry.
Bring to boil and simmer for 15 minutes.
Add chicken and server when warmed.
Do not overcook.
Serves 3 to 4.

PITA PIZZA PIE

1 package pita bread
1 6-oz. can tomato paste
4 cloves garlic, chopped finely
2 tablespoons dry onion
1 cup dried mushrooms
1/2 green bell pepper, diced
1/2 cup water
grated mozzarella cheese

Let mushrooms rehydrate in water for 15 minutes.
In pot, combine tomato paste and water along with spices and mushrooms over low heat. In another frying pan, sauté garlic and pepper.
Add garlic and green pepper to pot.
In lightly oiled frying pan, add pita, spread sauce and cheese, cover over low heat. Serve when cheese melts, and pita is slightly brown.
Serves 2.

BOEUF DE PROVENCE
WITH POTATOES

2 10-oz. cans cubed beef in sauce
3 tablespoons dried onion
(presoak with 1/4 cup water, do not drain)
3 to 4 cloves garlic
2 tablespoons capers
1 6-oz. can tomato paste
8-oz. can of black olives
1 teaspoon oregano
1 teaspoon Herbes de Provence
Mashed potato flakes, enough for 4 servings

Add all ingredients except potatoes to pot.
Add enough water to moisten.
Heat and simmer for 15 minutes, stirring.
Meanwhile, cook potatoes in separate pot
as per directions on package.
Serves 4.

PEPPERONI POTATOES

6 cups instant mashed potatoes
6 cups water
4 tablespoons olive oil or butter
1 green pepper, chopped
3 green onions, chopped
3 small carrots, chopped
6 ounces pepperoni
(can substitute salami or smoked sausage)
8 ounces sharp cheddar, cubed
garlic powder to taste

Bring water to a boil.
Add veggies and pepperoni,
and cook for a few minutes.
Stir in potatoes.
Remove from heat.
Fold in butter or olive
oil and garlic powder.
Add cheddar cheese and let
stand 10 minutes. Serves 4

THAI SHRIMP WRAPS

1 cup instant rice or Basmati rice
3 tablespoons dried onion
3 tablespoons coconut cream powder
or dried shredded coconut
2 tablespoons dried cilantro
2 teaspoons minced dried ginger
1/2 teaspoon garlic powder
2 5-oz. cans of shrimp
8 to 10 7 1/2-inch flour tortillas

Mix all dried ingredients in pot.
Add 1 cup boiling water.
Let stand covered for 6 minutes.
If using Basmati, add an extra cup
of water and cook until tender.
Add shrimp and juice and warm.
Heat individual tortillas in pan.
Add filling to tortilla,
turn in sides and roll up.
Serve immediately. Serves 2 to 3.

TURKEY WITH
CRANBERRY RICE

2 cups instant rice
3/4 cup dried mushrooms (rehydrate)
2 10-oz. cans turkey or freezedried equiv.
1 package turkey gravy mix
2/3 cup dried cranberries
2 teaspoons dried onions
1/2 teaspoon powdered bay leaves
1 teaspoon sage
1 small can water chestnuts (optional)

Add all ingredients, except turkey, to
5 cups boiling water. Simmer for 10
minutes. Add turkey with juice. Add
water if necessary. Remove from heat,
cover and let stand 10 minutes.
Serves 4.

Tuna Fettucini

2 6-oz. cans tuna packed in oil
1 lb. spinach fettucini noodles
1 package mushroom soup
2 tablespoons dried onions
2 teaspoons parsley flakes
1/2 teaspoon thyme
1/2 teaspoon basil
1 can sliced olives, drained
Romano cheese to garnish

Mix all dry ingredients. Cook soup, adding necessary amount of water to make a thick sauce. Add tuna, dried onions and herbs. Simmer for 10 minutes, stirring occasionally to keep from sticking. In separate pot boil pasta until tender. Drain and combine with sauce and olives. Simmer until eating temperature. Garnish with Romano cheese. Serve immediately. Serves 3 to 4.

Onion Quesadillas

1 red onion, cut into thin rings
4 flour tortillas (10 inches wide)
1 can refried beans
1 small can green chiles, chopped
1/4 lb. Monterey Jack cheese
4 green onions, chopped

Brown red onions in small amount of oil in non-stick frying pan for about 5 minutes. Remove. Brush tortillas on both sides with water. Place in frying pan. Spread beans and chiles over half of each tortilla. Top with red onions and cheese. Fold tortilla over filling. Cook until golden brown and cheese is melted. Garnish with chopped green onions. Serves 2.

Polenta with Tomato-Pepper Mushroom Sauce

6 cups water
1 teaspoon salt
2 cups polenta, or yellow corn meal
2 tablespoons butter
1/2 cup Parmesan cheese

Combine water and salt in deep pot and bring to boil. Reduce heat to simmer. Add polenta, stirring constantly. Cook until polenta is thickened. Transfer to an oiled bowl or flat pan. Let cool. Invert onto a dish and cut into portions when firm. Fry in a little olive oil and serve with butter and grated cheese or with sauce that follows.

SAUCE:

1 cup sun dried tomatoes (reconstituted)
1 small can tomato paste
1 large sweet red pepper
1 cup dried mushrooms
2 tablespoons olive oil
2 large cloves of garlic, chopped
2 teaspoons dried cilantro or parsley
1 teaspoon marjoram
salt and pepper

Saute reconstituted mushrooms and red pepper in olive oil. Add sun dried tomatoes, tomatoe paste and spices. Add enough water to make a sauce. Add salt and pepper to taste. Simmer for 15 minutes. Serve over polenta. Garnish with cheese. Serves 4.

Other variations:
Add eggplant, zucchini, or yellow onions to sauce. Leftover squares of polenta can be grilled for a rib-sticking breakfast.

Sweets

OATMEAL SHORTBREAD

1-1/2 cups unsifted flour
2/3 cup rolled oats
1 cup butter or margerine
2/3 cup brown sugar

Combine all ingredients and mix
with fingers until well blended.
Pat into a lighty greased pan.
Bake in oven at 300° or in camp
reflector oven for 30-40 minutes.
Cut into squares while still warm.
Cool in pan. Makes about 3 dozen 2-
inch squares.

TOOTSIE FUDGE BALLS

1 cup crunchy peanut butter
1/2 cup cocoa or carob powder
1/2 cup dry milk
1/2 cup raisins
1/4 cup chopped walnuts
1/8 cup wheat germ
1/4 cup honey

Mix all ingredients. Roll into small
balls, wrap and chill. Store in airtight
container on trail.

S'MORES

1 bag marshmellows,
1 box graham crackers
1 package chocolate bars

Toast marshmellow on a stick.
Place cooked marshmellow and chocolate
square between two graham crackers.
Eat. Make more.

RICE PUDDING

2 cups cooked rice
3 tablespoons milk powder
1/2 cup water
2 tablespoons sugar or brown sugar
2 tablespoons cooking oil
pinch of salt
1/2 teaspoon cinnamon
1 egg (substitute 1 teaspoon cornstarch)
1 tablespoon brandy
1/2 cup chopped dried apricots
   or pears or raisins
1 cup crushed ginger snaps or
   vanilla wafers

Oil pot and line with crushed cookies.
Mix milk powder, water, sugar, salt,
cinnamon, egg, brandy and fruit.
Add to rice. Add to cookie-lined pot, top
with remaining cookies.
Cook over low heat for 20 minutes.
Serves 3 to 4.

HARDY HARDTACK

5-1/2 cups whole wheat flour
1 teaspoon baking soda
2/3 cup cold water
2 eggs
2 cups molasses
1 teaspoon ginger
1 teaspoon cloves
1 cup raisins
2/3 cup melted butter

Combine baking soda, water and ginger.
Beat eggs, milk, molasses and butter.
Combine the two liquids.
To flour mixture add liquids. Add raisins.
Fold gently. Knead on floured surface.
Roll out to 1/4 inch. Cut into squares.
Bake at 350° for 15 minutes.

ILLUSTRATIONS

INDEX

Knott, Thomas 135
Konesberg 129
Kuna Ridge 98, 100

L

Lahontan Lakeland Empire 79
Lake Aloha 107, 114, 116
Lake Alpine 72-73
Lake Alpine Lodge 161
Lake Bigler 107
Lake Bonpland 107
Lake LeConte 114
Lake Lois 114
Lake Lucille 114, 116
Lake Margery 114, 116
Lake of the Woods 114, 116
Lake Schindell 114
Lake Tahoe 6, 106-107, 109, 116-117,
    121, 140-143
Lake Tahoe Visitors Authority 159
Lane Lake 82-83
Layton State Park 143
League to Save Lake Tahoe 107, 155
Leavitt Lake 83-84, 87
Leavitt Lake Pass 83-84
Leavitt Meadows 82-83, 87, 88
Leavitt Meadows Pack Station 82, 158
LeConte Falls 101
LeConte, Joseph 93
Lee Vining Creek 99
Lembert Dome 101, 102, 105
Leviathan Mine 62, 74
Leviathan Mine Road 127
Leviathan Peak 55, 75-76, 128
Lily Lake 111
Little Antelope Pack Station
    (business) 157
Little Antelope Pack Station 67,77,
    81-82, 85

Little Cottonwood Canyon 73-74
Little Walker River 79, 85-87
Llewellyn Falls 77, 81-82
Long Valley 81-82
Lookout Peak 72
Loope 127
Loope Canyon 73-74, 127
Loope, Dr. 127
Lost Cabin Mine 40, 121
Lower Blue Lake 42-43
Lower Echo Lake 114
Lower Fish Valley 81-82
Lower Gaylor Lake 99
Lower Kinney Lake 68
Lower Velma Lake 113
Luther Pass 8, 31-32, 140
Luther, Ira M. 140
Luther, M. 140
Lyell Canyon 100-101
Lyell Fork Tuolumne River 100
Lyell Meadow 100

M

M.S. Dixie 141
Mammals 146
Mammoth Lakes 101
Maps 163
Marklee, Jacob J. 124
Markleeville 54-55, 78-79, 124
Markleeville Creek 124
Markleeville General Store 124,162
Markleeville Lookout 73-74
Markleeville Peak 41-42, 59
Marla Bay 117, 141
Martin Meadows 35
Matterhorn Canyon 88
Matterhorn Peak 88
May Lake 104-105
May Lake High Sierra Camp 105

ORDERING INFORMATION

If your bookstore is out of **Alpine Trailblazer** or
doesn't carry it, you may order directly in two ways.

To pay by credit card:

Call 1-800-423-9949, seven days a week during business hours.

To pay by check:

Fill in the information requested on this form and send it to the address below with a
check or money order made payable to the **Diamond Valley Company**. Buy one book for
$14.95, or two books for $25.95, a 13% discount. *You may use the form, or supply
information on a separate piece of paper.* For larger orders, request a discount schedule
from the publisher.

ORDER FORM _____

NAME

ADDRESS

CITY, STATE, ZIP CODE

TELEPHONE: DATE:

1 book for $14.95	$_____
or 2 books for $25.95	$_____
priority shipping $3.50 for one or two books	$_____
sales tax, $1.23 for Calif. residents only *(1 book)*	$_____
sales tax, $2.14 *(2 books)*	$_____
Total	$_____

PUBLISHER: _____

Diamond Valley Company

89 Lower manzanita drive

MARKLEEVILLE, CA 96120

fax: 530-694-2740

e-mail: trailblazer@gbis.com

*The publisher would appreciate
receiving your comments and
suggestions so that we may
improve subsequent editions.*